# Reading Strategies
## for Mathematics

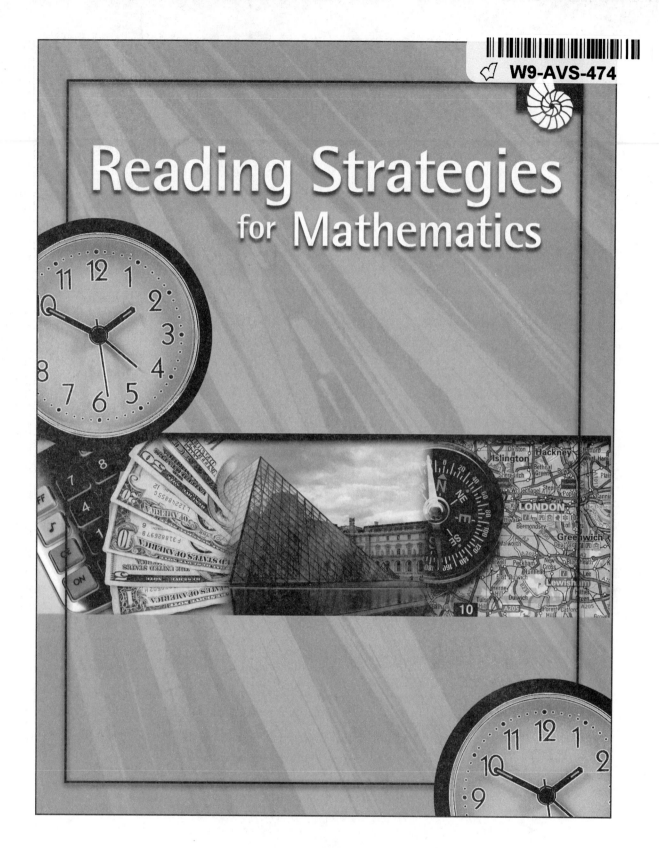

**Authors**

Trisha Brummer, M.S.Ed. and Stephanie Macceca, M.A.Ed.

# SHELL EDUCATION

**Editor**
Conni Medina

**Assistant Editor**
Leslie Huber, M.A.

**Senior Editor**
Lori Kamola, M.S.Ed.

**Editor-in-Chief**
Sharon Coan, M.S.Ed.

**Editorial Manager**
Gisela Lee, M.A.

**Consultant**
Judy Chambers, M.Ed.
1995 Recipient
Presidential Award for Excellence
in Math and Science Teaching

**Creative Director**
Lee Aucoin

**Cover Design**
Lee Aucoin

**Illustration Manager/Designer**
Timothy Bradley

**Print Production**
Kimberly Weber

**Interior Layout Designer**
Don Tran

**Publisher**
Corinne Burton, M.A.Ed.

**Shell Education**
5301 Oceanus Drive
Huntington Beach, CA 92649-1030
http://www.shelleducation.com
**ISBN 978-1-4258-0055-0**
©2008 Shell Education
Made in U.S.A

# Table of Contents

# Introduction: What Is Reading in Mathematics?

Reading is a complex act for humans. As Dechant (1991) outlines, it is a visual process that begins with one's ability to use one's vision to interpret graphic symbols. Reading requires great visual acuity. To read, one must be able to visually distinguish each letter, identify each letter, have a visual memory for each letter, and recode those letters so that one can recreate the letters, pronounce the letters, or associate sound with the letters. But, can one understand what the words mean? This is the essence of reading comprehension; to comprehend what is read, readers must be able to cognitively process the words by drawing meaning from their own experience and knowledge to understand the author's message. In essence, reading is a dialogue between the reader and the author, and during this "dialogue," the reader should generate questions to help anticipate meaning, search for information, respond intellectually and emotionally, and infer ideas from and explain further the content of the text.

## Everyone Should Teach Reading

The saying, "Every teacher is a teacher of reading" is well known but not always true. It is usually regarded as the task of the English or language arts teacher to guide students through the effective use of comprehension strategies as they read. Although students read in almost every subject area they study, content area teachers typically overlook the need for guiding students through their textbook-based and trade book-based reading tasks. Comprehension strategies best serve students when they are employed across the curricula and in the context of their actual learning. It is only then that students can independently use the strategy successfully when reading. Students typically read literature or fictional stories for English or language arts, but they will spend the majority of their adulthood reading nonfiction, expository writing. The strategies that students learn to comprehend literature are different from those they use for nonfiction. It is important to note that around the time students are in grades four and five, educators see a drop in reading achievement. At this time, students seem to lose interest in reading independently, spend less time reading for pleasure, and struggle more to read the materials required of them at school. It is for this reason that all teachers at all levels must actively pursue ways to greatly enhance their students' ability to understand reading material, and this can be accomplished by working directly with reading comprehension strategies.

## Mathematical Reading

The goal of literacy in mathematics is to develop in students a curiosity about the world around them. The study of mathematics should help students make better sense of the world in which they live. In order to understand their world, students must learn how to question their knowledge, methodology, skills, values, and attitude toward the world around them. Students must observe the world around them, ask questions, and then search to find the answers to those questions. Students usually look to their textbooks, often the only books they have for mathematics instruction, to find the answers to their questions, but this confines them to a realm that is often too abstract to understand. S. Gudder once said, "The essence of mathematics is not to make simple things complicated, but to make complicated things simple." Mathematicians would wholeheartedly agree, and yet mathematics remains a mystery to many of today's students. These students do not understand the significant role that mathematics plays in their adult lives, and they rarely see the link between reading and mathematics. By continually applying appropriate reading strategies to mathematics, students are able to bridge the gap between the two constructs, and ultimately, unite them for a better understanding of both.

# Introduction: What Is Reading in Mathematics? *(cont.)*

## Mathematical Reading *(cont.)*

Teachers present material from the book, and students ask questions, take notes, perhaps discuss the information, practice the concept with problems from the book, and usually take a test on the material they practiced. These students typically do not learn how to read the text effectively or independently to further their interest in and learning about any given subject. However, there is a tremendous jump in achievement when students are actively engaged in activities that go beyond the textbook. By introducing a wide variety of mathematics-based reading related to their studies, students learn that not all mathematical information comes from one textbook. Many people are interested in many topics in mathematics, and the reading material available reflects this. Expanding learning beyond the textbook both empowers students to become independent learners and exposes them to perspectives and topics they might otherwise overlook.

## Literacy Demands

The literacy needs of the 21st century are tremendous. Literacy was defined a century ago by one's ability to write one's name. A literate person could write his or her name, while an illiterate person could not. In the 1940s, one needed to be able to read at the eighth-grade level to function adequately in the factory setting. To be considered literate today, one needs to be able to successfully read at the 11th- or 12th-grade level as a part of workplace duties, leisure activities, and civic duty. This means a person should be able to read effectively, for example, the nutrition facts listed about the food he or she eats. The sidebar on this page is an example of the nutrition facts provided on a regular loaf of wheat bread.

## Nutrition Facts

Serving Size 1 slice (36g)
Servings Per Container 11

**Amount per Serving**

**Calories** 90          Calories from Fat 10

|  |  | %Daily Value* |
|---|---|---|
| **Total Fat** 1g | | 2% |
| Saturated Fat 0g | | 0% |
| Trans Fat 0g | | |
| **Cholesterol** 0mg | | 0% |
| **Sodium** 160mg | | 7% |
| **Total Carbohydrates** 18g | | 6% |
| Dietary Fiber 2g | | 8% |
| Sugars 2g | | |
| **Protein** 3g | | |
| Vitamin A | | 0% |
| Vitamin C | | 0% |
| Calcium | | 4% |
| Iron | | 6% |
| Thiamin | | 8% |
| Riboflavin | | 4% |
| Niacin | | 6% |
| Folate | | 6% |

*Percent Daily Values are based on a 2000 calorie diet.

**Ingredients:** Unbleached Enriched Flour [Wheat Flour, Malted Barley Flour, Reduced Iron, Niacin, Thiamin Mononitrate (Vitamin B1), Riboflavin (B2), Folic Acid], Water, Whole Wheat Flour, High Fructose Corn Syrup, Yeast, Cracked Wheat, Rye, Molasses, Extract of Raisins, Soybean Oil, Yellow Corn Grits, Salt, Nonfat Milk, Wheat Gluten, Brown Rice Oats, Monoglycerides, Soy Flour, Triticale, Grain Vinegar, Calcium Sulfate, Barley, Flaxseed, Millet, Soy Lechithin, Ascorbic Acid (Dough Container), Azodicarbonamide.

# Introduction: What Is Reading in Mathematics? *(cont.)*

## Literacy Demands *(cont.)*

In order to understand the information presented, the reader must understand the words *serving*, *per*, *percent*, and *values*. The reader also should be able to understand how to calculate percentages. He or she must be able to decipher between parentheses and brackets and understand what they mean when used together, as they are in the sample list of ingredients. Understanding the information on this label is not an easy task because of the complicated vocabulary. A strong reader with keen comprehension skills would think of a number of questions when reading the bread label: Does this bread contain enough fiber based on the number of grams and percentage listed? How many calories would I consume if I ate a sandwich using this bread? How many loaves of bread would I need to buy in order to make enough sandwiches to feed the 15 kids on my soccer team? Making decisions based on dietary needs or quantity becomes increasingly difficult without a solid foundation in mathematics. This is why teachers must incorporate the strategic teaching of reading comprehension strategies in content areas.

Perhaps the individual reading this label is diabetic. He or she must be able to determine the sugar and carbohydrate content of the food. Many individuals have set calorie limitations, depending on dietary needs. This is one of the many ways in which mathematics becomes a part of the everyday lives of today's students. It is also why mathematics teachers must incorporate the strategic teaching of reading comprehension strategies into their lessons.

We have entered a new era in education, and this era is deeply tied to the technological advances that have permeated our modern lives. Today, children can use a cell phone to take a picture before they can speak. A typical three-year-old can turn on a computer and begin a game program without assistance from an adult. Students in school can use the Internet and online libraries to access information from remote locations. They can interview experts in faraway locations through email. Now, more than ever, it is the content-area teacher's responsibility and duty to prepare students for the reading demands of our technological age. In order to become effective and efficient readers, students need to use comprehension strategies automatically and independently. Students need teacher guidance to help them become independent readers and learners so that they not only understand what they read but can also question it and create beyond it.

# Introduction:
# Motivating Students to Read

One of the easiest and most effective ways to improve comprehension in mathematics is to promote extensive reading outside of class. Students who frequently read a wide variety of materials have better vocabularies and better reading comprehension skills. As Ryder and Graves (2003) point out, wide reading fosters automaticity in students because it exposes them to more words in different contexts, provides them with knowledge on a variety of topics, and promotes lifelong reading habits.

Unfortunately, many students do very little reading, and some do not read at all outside of school. It is for this reason that teachers, especially mathematics teachers, must encourage and provide many opportunities for students to read engaging materials. Some students dislike reading the literature-based stories in language arts instruction, and they, in turn, seem to dislike reading in general. That very same child may love reading books that are more interactive and involve counting or patterning, so it is important to remember that reading skills can and should be developed when teaching mathematics.

A teacher's attitude toward reading, especially pleasure reading outside of school, has a tremendous effect on the students in the classroom. Teachers who talk enthusiastically about books they have read and who model reading as an enjoyable and fulfilling experience foster a love of reading in their students. Teachers who can recommend books that are particularly engaging and interesting can increase student motivation tremendously. Mathematics teachers should have an intimate knowledge of mathematics-based reading materials for a wide range of reading abilities, so they can recommend books to any student to read outside of class.

## The Classroom Library

The first step is to set up a classroom library. Why is it important to have a classroom library? According to Lesley Mandel Morrow (2003), president of the International Reading Association (2003–04), research indicates that children in classrooms with book collections read 50 percent more books than children in classrooms without such collections. Teachers should work with the school librarian or media specialist and parent organizations to build a sizeable mathematics collection for their classrooms. Go to used book stores, library sales, and garage sales to gather inexpensive, quality materials. Locate scholarly articles online, print them, and place them in thin folders to preserve their quality. Be sure to look for mathematical trade books. Invite students to locate and donate materials they find on relevant mathematics topics. Students should have a wide variety of materials about:

- **Numbers and Operations:** understanding numbers, the ways of representing them, their relationships, and number systems

- **Measurement:** the measurable attributes of objects and the various units, systems, and processes of measurement

- **Geometry:** the characteristics and properties of two- and three-dimensional shapes and the mathematical arguments about their relationships

- **Data Analysis and Probability:** involvement in the collection, organization, and display of data as it relates to a given topic

- **Algebra:** patterns, relations, and functions

# Introduction:
# Motivating Students to Read (cont.)

## The Classroom Library (cont.)

The reading materials should be housed in bookcases that provide easy access for students to use as needed. Use tubs to hold magazines and articles on related mathematics topics. Most importantly, provide reading materials for a wide range of reading skills. Some students read at a much lower level than others, so include many picture books in addition to articles from mathematical journals. Students will be better able to incorporate their new learning through independent reading into their existing prior knowledge if the materials are organized in terms of the different mathematics strands: Numbers and Operations, Measurement, Geometry, Data Analysis and Probability, and Algebra.

Once the materials are in place, be sure to create opportunities to incorporate them into mathematics instruction. Create inquiry-based research assignments in which students can use classroom library materials to independently learn more about different topics.

Also, encourage wide reading by making free voluntary reading a regular classroom activity. If students are not doing any reading outside of school, the school should provide some time for students to read in class. It may be nearly impossible to imagine blocking out any time for silent reading in today's demanding classrooms, but as Stephen Krashen makes clear in his "88 Generalizations about Free Voluntary Reading," more reading leads to better reading, faster reading, better writing, more writing, and better language acquisition.

# Introduction: The Reading Process

Mathematics teachers can easily optimize the use of reading materials with students by utilizing the three-part framework of the reading process to facilitate learning. Break reading assignments into three comprehension-building steps: before reading, during reading, and after reading. It is important to note that what teachers do during each stage of the reading process is crucial to their students' learning.

## Before Reading

Prior to beginning a reading assignment, engage in a variety of activities in the hopes of reducing any uncertainty involved in the reading task. These activities include generating interest in the topic, building and activating prior knowledge, and setting the purpose for reading.

Mathematics teachers who motivate students and create interest prior to assigning the reading improve their students' overall comprehension. Students who are more motivated to read are more engaged and actively involved in the process of learning than those who are not motivated to read. Motivated readers are also more likely to have better long-term recall of what they read.

Mathematics teachers can motivate students by assessing their prior knowledge. Knowing students' background knowledge on a topic makes it easier to build on and activate that knowledge during reading. The mind holds information in the form of frameworks called schemata, and as we learn new information, we store it in a framework of what we already know. Teachers who build on and activate students' prior knowledge before reading prepare students to more efficiently comprehend the material they will be reading.

Prior to reading, teachers should prepare students to read by setting a purpose for the reading task. There are a number of different purposes a student can have for a reading assignment: understand a new mathematical concept, learn the steps of a mathematical process, predict what will happen, learn new vocabulary, summarize the information, and so on. Students need to know what their purpose is as they read because it helps them focus their efforts. In doing so, teachers can guide the students' search for meaning as they read.

Mathematics teachers should also take the time to introduce key concepts and vocabulary prior to reading. In doing so, they help the students read the selection more fluently, with greater automaticity, and with greater comprehension—all of which lead to greater recall of the information.

Finally, teachers should establish in their students a metacognitive awareness for the task of reading. Students should be prompted to be aware of what they are thinking and doing as they are reading. Developing metacognitive awareness allows students to better understand the strategies necessary for effective learning. It also enables students to take control of their own learning and makes them more independent readers and learners.

# Introduction:
# The Reading Process *(cont.)*

## Before-Reading Activities

Examples of before-reading activities are as follows:

- Scan visual aids such as diagrams of pizzas and birthday cakes.

- Preview text structure for titles such as *Fractions* and subheadings such as *Adding and Subtracting Fractions* and *Multiplying and Dividing Fractions.*

- Skim the reading to activate prior knowledge. *What, if anything, do I already know about fractions?*

- Review unknown vocabulary or preview any bolded words in the margins or within the text. *Let's talk about the bolded words in the margin: numerator, denominator, improper fraction, and mixed number.*

- Discuss, activate, assess, and build on background knowledge about the topic. *What can you share about your knowledge of fractions?*

- Brainstorm related ideas. *How could we cut a pizza to show $\frac{1}{2}$?*

- Generate questions that may be answered in the reading. *What is the difference between 0.5 and 50%?*

- Predict what will happen. *How many times would I have to cut a cake in half to feed 12 people?*

- Anticipate the contents of the reading. *What will this section tell us about how fractions can be manipulated?*

- Hold purpose-setting conversations. *What should we be able to do when we have finished this section, and how does it apply to everyday life?*

## During Reading

During reading, students are actively reading text aloud or silently. During this stage of the reading process, students are engaged in answering questions (either self- or teacher-generated), monitoring their comprehension of the text, clarifying the purpose of reading, visualizing the information, and building connections.

Most often, students are engaged in answering questions while they read. Proficient readers self-question as they read to make sure they understand the reading material. In addition, students search for the answers to questions they may have generated prior to reading. As students process the text, they begin to infer what the author intended and begin to generalize about the specific details in the information provided. They also look for support for the predictions they have made.

Students are involved in monitoring and regulating their reading abilities while they are actively reading. If a section of the text is confusing, students need to know that they can reread the section, use fix-up strategies to help them understand what they are puzzled by, or adjust the speed of reading to suit their purposes and to suit the difficulty of the text. Thus, students must monitor their own reading strategies and make modifications as needed.

# Introduction:
# The Reading Process (cont.)

## During Reading (cont.)

In addition to monitoring their reading abilities, students are also "solving" words as they actively read. If they do not know what a word means, they use the context clues or word parts to decode the meaning of the word. As students attend to vocabulary needs, they also observe the text structure and features as they read, which helps them organize the new information while they read.

During reading, mathematics teachers can focus students' attention on the objectives of the reading task. Students may adjust their purposes for reading based on the information they are reading and on their prior knowledge.

Proficient readers actively work to create images in their mind that represent the concepts in the reading material. Mathematics teachers should engage the students in creating mental images to help them comprehend the material as they are reading. This promotes greater recall of the information and engages the students in the reading process.

While students are reading, they are in the process of connecting the new information they are learning to their existing schemata. Therefore, mathematics teachers should be actively involved in helping students make connections between what they already know and what they are learning. This prepares them for the synthesis of the information. Teachers can be instrumental in helping students relate to the material.

## During-Reading Activities

Examples of during-reading activities are as follows:

- Reread to clarify confusion. *The word variable is confusing, so let's reread this part.*
- Solve words. *What are polygons? Which parts of the word do you recognize?*
- Monitor and regulate reading. *This word problem is confusing. What should we do?*
- Self-question to monitor understanding. *Are we ready to explain the difference between $3\frac{1}{3}$ and $\frac{10}{3}$?*
- Seek answers to questions. *Should we use a fraction or a decimal to solve the problem?*
- Observe text structure. *This subheading, "Looking for Patterns," tells me that we are going to look for patterns of the shapes below.*
- Support predictions. *I was right because the next shape in the pattern is a triangle.*
- Make connections between ideas and between new information and prior knowledge. *Think about each of the 4 pieces of a pizza as $\frac{1}{4}$.*
- Build on prior knowledge. *I know that 1,000 is bigger than 100, so the next place value might be the thousands place.*
- Stimulate discussion. *How can we take what we know about whole numbers and use it to help us understand integers?*
- Focus on an objective. *Let's list the steps we take in solving an equation.*
- Infer author's intentions. *I think the author uses this step to help us build to the next step.*
- Generalize about specific details. *Even numbers are always divisible by 2.*
- Visualize content. *Let's imagine a coordinate plane.*
- Adjust purpose for reading. *This section tells us about the different shapes. Let's compare them as we read.*

# Introduction:
## The Reading Process *(cont.)*

## After Reading

Students expand their understanding of the material after reading the text. During the final stage of the reading process, students build connections among the bits of information they have read, enabling them to deepen their understanding and reflect upon what they have learned.

After reading, students need the teacher to guide them through follow-up experiences so they can reflect on what they have read. During reflection, students can contemplate the new information, clarify new ideas, refine their thinking, and connect what they have learned to other ideas to synthesize the new information. Teachers should spend time revisiting the text with students to demonstrate that the reading experience is not a single event.

Also, teachers should have students find the main idea and distinguish the most important ideas from less important ideas. This enables them to prioritize and summarize what they have read.

After reading, teachers generally assess what students have learned. Students answer questions about what they have learned, and teachers generally use their answers to determine whether the students can move on or need additional instruction. Teachers can take advantage of additional after-reading activities to deepen students' comprehension of the text.

After students have read, they are able to engage in higher-level thinking tasks. Students can use critical thinking to evaluate the quality or validity of the material, or they can synthesize what they have learned by integrating their new knowledge with their prior knowledge. They can also analyze what they have read by closely examining the text characteristics specific to the genre.

## After-Reading Activities

Examples of after-reading activities are as follows:

- Reread to review information and locate specific information. *What is the order of place values?*
- Confirm predictions. *I was right that the prefix* hex- *told me that the shape has 6 sides.*
- Discuss what was understood and share information. *I was right that a variable can be any letter:* x, y, a, b, *etc.*
- Clarify meaning. *Who can explain perpendicular lines?*
- Relate the reading to the reader. *Think about what you would use to measure your book vs. a football field.*
- Summarize what was read. *Numbers are made up of the digits 0, 1, 2, 3, 4, 5, 6, 7, 8, and 9.*
- Synthesize new information. *Now I understand the relationship between a square and a rectangle.*
- Analyze different elements of the text. *This diagram helped me understand the equation* $a = \frac{1}{2}bh$.
- Evaluate the quality or accuracy of the text. *How well does the author support his or her explanation of slope for a linear function?*
- Generate new questions. *How can we apply this mathematics concept to our everyday lives?*
- Assess what was learned. *Let's classify these angles as scalene or obtuse.*

# Introduction: Explicit Instruction of Reading Comprehension Strategies

If mathematics teachers were asked how they improve their students' reading skills, the majority would most likely struggle to answer the question. Good teachers use many strategies to enhance students' reading comprehension, and it is helpful to identify which strategies they use in order to explain why each technique successfully improves their students' skills. Even more important is the explicit instruction of the individual strategies, including modeling, guided practice, and independent practice. These steps ensure that students learn to independently and consistently use a wide variety of reading comprehension strategies for a broad range of reading experiences.

Teaching students the strategies to improve their comprehension is nothing new to educators. Research has demonstrated that students greatly benefit from the direct instruction of reading comprehension strategies while reading a text (Duke and Pearson 2002), (Block 1999; Dole, Brown, and Trathen 1996; Durkin 1978/1979; Pressley and Afflerbach 1995, as cited by Kragler, Walker, and Martin 2005). Simply put, strategy instruction is an effective means of assisting students in improving comprehension.

The National Reading Panel Report (2000), commissioned by the U.S. Congress to evaluate research in the area of reading, identified a number of effective comprehension strategies. Pressley (2000) echoes these findings. These strategies include vocabulary development, prediction skills (including inference), the building of prior knowledge, think-alouds, visual representations, summarization, and questioning. This book provides a detailed explanation of each strategy and describes a number of activities that mathematics teachers can incorporate into their lessons.

Students also need to develop their metacognitive skills while reading and learning in mathematics. Scholars agree that metacognition plays a significant role in reading comprehension (e.g., Baker and Brown 1984; Garner 1987; Gourgey 1998; Hacker 1998; Mastropieri and Scruggs 1997; Mayer 1998; Paris, Wasik, and Turner 1991; Schraw 1998, as cited by Baker 2002). Research shows that teachers should foster metacognition and comprehension monitoring during comprehension instruction because in doing so, students will be able to monitor and self-regulate their ability to read. "Developing engaged readers involves helping students to become both strategic and aware of the strategies they use to read" (McCarthy, Hoffman, and Galda 1999, as cited by Baker 2002).

It is important to note that educators should never take a "one size fits all" approach to teaching reading comprehension. Some strategies work for some students and other strategies work for other students, just as some strategies work best with certain types of reading material and other strategies work best with other types of reading material. The most important thing to remember when trying to improve reading comprehension in students is that the skill level, group dynamic, and make-up of the students should determine the approach to take.

# Introduction: Explicit Instruction
# of Reading Comprehension Strategies *(cont.)*

## The Steps Involved in Explicit Instruction of Reading Comprehension Strategies

According to Duke and Pearson (2002), research supports that a balanced approach to teaching reading comprehension is more than teaching students specific reading strategies and providing opportunities to read. Teachers should begin with direct explanation and instruction of how to use the strategy so that after a series of steps, students will be able to use the strategy independently. The following are the five steps for explicit instruction of comprehension strategies:

1. **Provide an exact description of the strategy and explain when and how it should be used.** Teachers need to explain what the strategy is called, why students should use it, what it helps them understand, and how often students should use it.

2. **Provide modeling of the strategy.** Teachers should model how to use the strategy when students are in the process of reading. Students can also model the strategy while the teacher reinforces an explanation of how the strategy is being used.

3. **Provide opportunities for collaborative use of the strategy in action.** Teachers and students should work together and share their use of the strategy while they are reading.

4. **Lead guided practice sessions using the strategy, and allow for a gradual release of responsibility from the teacher to the student.** At this stage, teachers can remind students of how to use the strategy and of the steps involved, but teachers should allow students to work on the technique independently.

5. **Encourage students' independent use of the strategy.** In the final stage, teachers might gently remind students of the name of the strategy, but the students should be using the technique automatically and independently.

Duke and Pearson (2002) emphasize the importance of remembering that students need to be able to use more than one comprehension strategy to understand a reading selection. Throughout the five phases, other strategies should be referenced and modeled for the students. When working with reading materials in mathematics, teachers should use the very same techniques to introduce a new learning strategy to students as they would during a language arts or an English class. Research shows that students only master the use of reading comprehension strategies when instruction follows the five steps listed above. When covering mathematics topics, teachers must take the time to allow students to master the strategy so that they can become independent readers.

# Introduction: What Great Teachers Do

Many mathematics teachers use a variety of strategies that go beyond simply answering the questions at the end of the chapter. Research shows, however, that there is a big difference between teaching reading comprehension strategies well and teaching them in a dynamic, ingenious way that motivates and excites students about reading and learning. Through research, observations, and conversations with teachers who have been successful with the direct instruction of reading comprehension strategies, Keene (2002) has identified five traits specific to outstanding and consistently effective teachers. What makes these teachers effective?

1. **They take the time to understand each strategy in their own reading.** Reading about the techniques and activities is not enough. Great teachers of reading comprehension strategies take the time to figure out how to use and understand every strategy with the texts they are reading. In doing so, they increase their own metacognitive skills and can better articulate their own thinking during reading.

2. **They incorporate reading comprehension strategy instruction into predictable daily, weekly, and monthly activities.** Effective teachers of reading comprehension strategies set goals for strategy learning and create a predictable schedule to ensure that those goals are met. These teachers set aside time to work more intensively with small groups as needed. They also allocate time for students to reflect on their progress toward the goals they set.

3. **They ask students to apply each comprehension strategy to a wide variety of texts and text levels in different contexts.** Great teachers use beautifully written texts with challenging and profound themes that can be read in their entirety in a mini-lesson. For example, they ask students to summarize the textbook and a short story, to use sensory images in poetry and expository essays, and to use background knowledge to understand a biography and the letters to the editor. In order to comprehend actively and assertively, students must read from texts with appropriately challenging words and concepts.

4. **They vary the size of groupings for strategy instruction.** Changing the group size and configuration helps teachers focus on different goals during comprehension strategy instruction.

   **Large groups are best for:**

   - introducing a new strategy

   - modeling think-alouds to show children how good readers use the strategy

   - practicing think-alouds with new genres, and allowing students to share their experiences using the strategy

   **Small groups are best for:**

   - providing more intensive instruction for students who need it

   - introducing gifted students to the strategy so that they can apply it independently to more challenging texts and to new genres

   - introducing new activities that enable students to share their thinking (maps, charts, thinking notebooks, sketches, etc.)

   - allowing students to discuss books and comprehension strategies without teacher involvement

# Introduction:
# What Great Teachers Do *(cont.)*

**Conferences are best for:**

- checking the student's understanding of how to apply the strategy he or she is studying to his or her own books

- providing intensive strategy instruction to a text that may be particularly challenging to the student

- coaching a child in how he or she might reveal his or her thinking to others

- pushing a child to use a strategy to think more deeply than he or she might have imagined possible

5. **They gradually release the responsibility for the application of a comprehension strategy to the students.** Great teachers follow the steps involved in the explicit instruction of reading comprehension strategies (Duke and Pearson 2002): over several weeks, teachers provide thorough explanations of the strategy, model how to use it, allow for group work with the strategy, transition to more independent use, and then release the responsibility to the students.

# Introduction: What Do Good Readers Do When They Read?

Duke and Pearson (2002) have established that good readers:

- **read** actively

- **set goals** for their reading tasks and constantly **evaluate** whether the text and their reading of it is meeting their goals

- **preview** the text prior to reading, noting the **text organization and structure** to locate the sections most relevant to their reading goals

- **make predictions** about what is to come in the text

- **read selectively**, continually making decisions about their reading process: what to read carefully, what to read quickly, what to skim, what not to read, and what to reread

- **construct, revise, and question the meanings they develop** as they read

- **determine the meanings of unfamiliar or unknown words and concepts** in the text

- **draw from, compare, and integrate their prior knowledge** with the material in the text

- **consider the authors of the text**, their styles, beliefs, intentions, historical perspectives, and so on

- **monitor their understanding of the text**, making adjustments in their reading as necessary and dealing with inconsistencies or gaps as needed

- **evaluate the text's quality and value**, and interact with the text in multiple ways, both intellectually and emotionally

- **read different kinds of texts differently**

- **construct and revise summaries** of what they have read when reading expository texts

- **think about the text before, during, and after reading**

- **feel satisfied and productive** when reading, even though comprehension is a consuming, continuous, and complex activity

Mathematics teachers can easily incorporate the same techniques that language arts teachers have used for years to help students become more strategic and skilled readers and to help them comprehend the mathematics materials they encounter. Teachers will find the job of using the mathematics textbook much easier if every student has the skills of a good reader.

# Introduction:
# How to Use This Book

This book includes a variety of strategies that can be used within mathematics lessons to improve students' reading comprehension skills: promoting word consciousness, analysis of word parts, activating knowledge through vocabulary development, using and building prior knowledge, predicting and inferring, think-alouds and comprehension monitoring, questioning, summarizing, using visual representations and mental imagery, using text structure and text features, and multiple reading comprehension strategy instruction.

Each section opens with an overview of current research in that area to emphasize the importance of that particular reading comprehension skill. It also includes a clear and detailed definition of the skill, suggestions for instruction, and best practices. This information provides teachers with the solid foundation of knowledge to provide deeper, more meaningful instruction to their students.

Following each skill overview are a variety of instructional strategies to improve students' comprehension in that area. Each strategy in the book includes the definition and purpose of the strategy, the research basis for the strategy, and the reasons why the strategy is effective in improving comprehension. The grade-level spans for which the strategy is most appropriate (1–2, 3–5, or 6–8) and the language arts standards that are addressed are listed. A detailed description of the strategy includes any special preparation that might be needed and extension ideas where appropriate. Finally, suggestions for differentiating instruction are provided for English language learners (ELLs), students reading below grade level, and gifted students. Following the strategy descriptions are grade-level examples of how the strategy is applied to mathematics.

A blank template of the graphic organizer or activity page is included as a reproducible where applicable as well as on the accompanying CD-ROM.

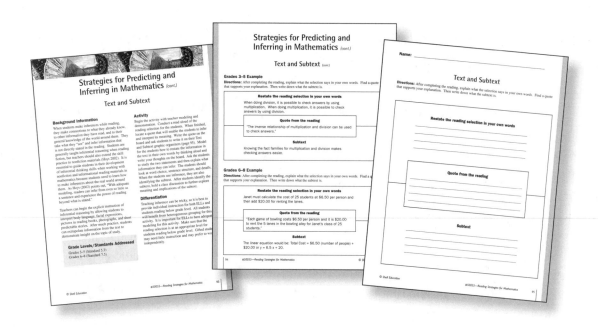

# Introduction: Correlation to Standards

## Correlation to Standards

The No Child Left Behind (NCLB) legislation mandates that all states adopt academic standards that identify the skills students will learn in kindergarten through grade 12. While many states had already adopted academic standards prior to NCLB, the legislation set requirements to ensure the standards were detailed and comprehensive.

Standards are designed to focus instruction and guide adoption of curricula. Standards are statements that describe the criteria necessary for students to meet specific academic goals. They define the knowledge, skills, and content students should acquire at each level. Standards are also used to develop standardized tests to evaluate students' academic progress.

In many states today, teachers are required to demonstrate how their lessons meet state standards. State standards are used in the development of Shell Education products, so educators can be assured that they meet the academic requirements of each state.

## How to Find Your State Correlations

Shell Education is committed to producing educational materials that are research- and standards-based. In this effort, all products are correlated to the academic standards of the 50 states, the District of Columbia, and the Department of Defense Dependent Schools. A correlation report customized for your state can be printed directly from the following website: **http://www.shelleducation.com**. If you require assistance in printing correlation reports, please contact Customer Service at 1-800-877-3450.

## McREL Compendium

Shell Education uses the Mid-continent Research for Education and Learning (McREL) Compendium to create standards correlations. Each year, McREL analyzes state standards and revises the compendium. By following this procedure, McREL is able to produce a general compilation of national standards.

Each reading comprehension strategy assessed in this book is based on one or more McREL content standards. The chart on pages 20–21 shows the McREL standards that correlate to each lesson used in the book. To see a state-specific correlation, visit the Shell Education website at **http://www.shelleducation.com**.

## Identifying Learning Objectives and Goals

When teaching a lesson that involves mathematics reading, the first step is to identify the learning objectives and goals for the lesson. The teacher should identify the goals of the lesson and discuss them directly with the students, because understanding the expectations and purpose of the lesson will help them to better gauge their own learning. Some of these goals may address language arts standards as well as mathematics standards. This is the first step in helping students develop the metacognitive skills necessary for self-monitoring. Planning for mathematics reading lessons with the goals in mind allows teachers to determine their objectives and address the learning standards required by the school district, state, and nation. As a result, teachers naturally build into their lessons a means of assessing students' learning.

# Introduction: Correlation to Standards (cont.)

| Grades | Objective | Pages |
|--------|-----------|-------|
| 1–2 | 5.1—Uses mental images based on pictures and print to aid in comprehension of text | 49–52, 167–168, 169–172 |
| 1–2 | 5.2—Uses meaning clues to aid comprehension and make predictions about content | 90–92, 96–99, 128–130, 173–174 |
| 1–2 | 5.4—Uses basic elements of structural analysis | 37–39 |
| 1–2 | 5.6—Understands level-appropriate sight words and vocabulary | 26–28 |
| 1–2 | 5.7—Uses self-correction strategies | 110–111, 112–113, 114–115, 116–117, 118–120, 121, 122–123 |
| 1–2 | 7.1—Uses reading skills and strategies to understand a variety of informational texts | 68–71, 183–184, 185 |
| 1–2 | 7.2—Understands the main idea and supporting details of simple expository information | 103–104 |
| 1–2 | 7.3—Summarizes information found in texts | 80–83, 84–87, 147–148, 149–151, 155–156, 157, 175–176, 177, 186, 188–191, 192–193 |
| 1–2 | 7.4—Relates new information to prior knowledge and experience | 56–59, 68–71, 80–83, 84–87, 116–117, 118–120, 169–172 |
| 1–2 | 8.2—Makes contributions in class and group discussions | 131–134, 135 |
| 3–5 | 5.1—Previews text | 90–92 |
| 3–5 | 5.2—Establishes a purpose for reading | 90–92, 167–168 |
| 3–5 | 5.3—Makes, confirms, and revises simple predictions about what will be found in a text | 29–31, 32–34, 93–95, 96–99, 100–102, 128–130, 173–174 |
| 3–5 | 5.4—Uses phonetic and structural analysis techniques, syntactic structure, and semantic context to decode unknown words | 37–39, 40–42, 43–45, 60–63 |
| 3–5 | 5.5—Uses a variety of context clues to decode unknown words | 29–31, 32–34, 118–120, 122–123 |
| 3–5 | 5.6—Uses word reference materials to determine the meaning, pronunciation, and derivations of unknown words | 40–42, 49–52, 53–55, 60–63 |
| 3–5 | 5.7—Understands level-appropriate reading vocabulary | 26–28, 49–52 |
| 3–5 | 5.8—Monitors own reading strategies and makes modifications as needed | 110–111, 112–113, 114–115, 116–117, 118–120, 121, 122–123 |
| 3–5 | 7.1—Uses reading skills and strategies to understand a variety of informational texts | 68–71, 72–75, 76–79, 80–83, 84–87 |

# Introduction:
## Correlation to Standards (cont.)

| Grades | Objective | Pages |
|---|---|---|
| 3–5 | 7.3—Uses text organizers to determine the main ideas and to locate information in a text | 188–191, 192–193 |
| 3–5 | 7.4—Uses the various parts of a book to locate information | 183–184, 185 |
| 3–5 | 7.5—Summarizes and paraphrases information in texts | 147–148, 149–151, 155–156, 157, 158–161, 175–176, 177, 186 |
| 3–5 | 7.6—Uses prior knowledge and experience to understand and respond to new information | 56–59, 68–71, 72–75, 76–79, 80–83, 84–87, 103–104, 116–117, 169–172 |
| 3–5 | 7.7—Understands structural patterns or organization in informational texts | 187 |
| 3–5 | 8.2—Asks questions in class | 131–134, 135, 136, 137, 138–140, 141, 142–143 |
| 3–5 | 9.1—Understands different messages conveyed through visual media | 178 |
| 6–8 | 5.1—Establishes and adjusts purposes for reading | 90–92, 96–99, 100–102, 173–174 |
| 6–8 | 5.2—Uses word origins and derivations to understand word meaning | 29–31, 32–34, 40–42, 43–45, 60–63, 167–168 |
| 6–8 | 5.3—Uses a variety of strategies to extend reading vocabulary | 26–28, 29–31, 32–34, 49–52, 53–55, 60–63 |
| 6–8 | 5.4—Uses specific strategies to clear up confusing parts of a text | 32–34, 110–111, 112–113, 114–115, 116–117, 118–120, 121, 122–123 |
| 6–8 | 7.1—Uses reading skills and strategies to understand a variety of informational texts | 68–71, 72–75, 76–79, 80–83, 84–87, 187 |
| 6–8 | 7.3—Summarizes and paraphrases information in texts | 147–148, 149–151, 152–154, 157, 158–161, 175–176, 177, 186, 188–191 |
| 6–8 | 7.4—Uses new information to adjust and extend personal knowledge base | 56–59, 68–71, 72–75, 76–79, 80–83, 84–87, 103–104, 116–117 |
| 6–8 | 7.5—Draws conclusions and makes inferences based on explicit and implicit information in texts | 93–95 |
| 6–8 | 8.2—Asks questions to seek elaboration and clarification of ideas | 131–134, 135, 136, 137, 138–140, 141, 142–143 |
| 6–8 | 9.1—Understands a variety of messages conveyed by visual media | 178 |

# Developing Vocabulary in Mathematics

## What Is Vocabulary?

What comes to mind when you hear the word *vocabulary*? For most, the word suggests a list of words ready for use in one's speech and writing. Educators and researchers in the field of reading have long recognized that vocabulary knowledge plays an integral role in a student's ability to comprehend reading material. Students with wider vocabularies find it easier to comprehend more of what they are reading than do those with limited vocabularies. Moreover, students who have strong vocabularies have less difficulty learning unfamiliar words because those words are more likely to be related to words that students already know (Rupley, Logan, and Nichols 1999).

As Nagy and Scott (2000) point out, for many people, the word vocabulary suggests a reductionist attitude toward word learning. The term vocabulary begs the reader to look just at words and their meanings, rather than at how the words are part of the overall reading process. The term vocabulary suggests that students learn words by memorizing short definitions or sentences. This limited perception about vocabulary, combined with the traditional and unsound methods of introducing words and asking students to look them up in the dictionary, goes against all that is known about the reading process. The process of using word knowledge to comprehend reading is rather complex and merits much discussion, particularly because most mathematics texts introduce a large number of vocabulary words that are unknown to the reader. Some high school texts contain an estimated 3,000 words that are unfamiliar to high school students (Lapp, Flood, and Farnan 1996).

## Levels of Word Knowledge

Researchers have established that there are different levels of word knowledge: *unknown*, *acquainted*, and *established* (Beck and McKeown 1991, as cited by Lapp, Flood, and Farnan 1996 and Ryder and Graves 2003). *Unknown* words are words that students neither recognize nor understand. Few kindergartners are able to define *histogram* (a type of bar graph). *Acquainted* words are those that students may recognize but must consciously think about to determine their meanings. Fourth graders are acquainted with the word *function*, but they may not be able to define it in detail. *Established* words are those words that the students recognize and can define easily and automatically. The word *polygon* should be well established in the vocabularies of every eighth grader.

The goal is to move new mathematics vocabulary into the established level for students so they can use the words in their own speech and writing. It is not enough for students to be acquainted with *quadrilateral*—the goal is for students to use the term easily when speaking and writing. To achieve this, teachers must expose students to the word a number of times and in a variety of contexts.

Knowing a word completely involves a number of skills: recognizing the word automatically; knowing the denotations, connotations, synonyms, antonyms, metaphors, and analogies for the word; associating the word with different experiences; and being able to explain one's understanding of the nuances of the word. Obviously, students cannot learn all of these skills with only a single exposure to the word (Lapp, Flood, and Farnan 1996). Word learning is an incremental process—a series of encounters that leads to mastery of the word. Sometimes brief instruction just before or after reading is all that students need to develop a thorough understanding of an unknown word.

## Word-Learning Tasks

In addition to different levels of word knowledge, there are different word-learning tasks that students engage in. Lapp, Flood, and Farnan (1996) categorize word learning into six distinct tasks:

- **Learning to Read Known Words**—Students may already have words in their oral vocabularies, but they may not recognize them in print. There is no need to teach the meanings of these words because students already know and understand them when they hear them; they just cannot read them. For example, mathematics students may have heard the word *quadratic*, but they may not recognize it in print.

- **Learning New Meanings for Known Words**—If the new meanings do not represent new and difficult concepts, teachers should acknowledge the known meaning, give the new meaning, and note the similarities between the meanings. Mathematics students usually recognize the word *square*, and may associate it with the shape, but they may not know that it also refers to multiplying a number by itself.

- **Learning New Words Representing Known Concepts**—Sometimes the words are not in the students' oral or reading vocabularies, but they do have prior knowledge of the concept. For example, mathematics students may not know the word *nonlinear*, but they know *non* and *line*, so the concept of nonlinear is present. Most words that students learn in middle school are of this type.

- **Learning New Words for New Concepts**— When students do not know the words or the concepts associated with the word, they have the demanding task of learning both. For these words, it is best to activate as much prior knowledge as possible with the students. For example, mathematics students probably have never heard of the word *asymptotes* and will need to develop the background knowledge to understand it.

- **Clarifying and Enriching the Meanings of Known Words**—As students become more sophisticated with their vocabularies, they begin to learn the nuances involved in words with varying shades of meaning. In mathematics, students will learn to distinguish *perimeter* from *circumference*.

- **Moving Words into Students' Expressive Vocabularies**—It is one thing to know a word, to recognize it, to know what it means, and to understand its shades of meaning. It is another task to use the word in speech or in writing.

# Developing Vocabulary in Mathematics *(cont.)*

## Vocabulary Instruction Should...

Typically, teachers focus on teaching specific words and their definitions in vocabulary instruction, but this is not the most effective method because of the complexity of word knowledge. Instead, students should be invited to build on their previous understandings of words to learn new meanings and nuances, to connect words to greater concepts, to associate words with other related words, to categorize words in unique and useful ways, and to enjoy using language creatively to express themselves and their ideas.

Blachowicz and Fisher (2000) feel that reading research suggests four main principles to guide vocabulary instruction. Students should:

1. Be active in developing their understanding of words and ways to learn them

2. Personalize word learning

3. Be immersed in words

4. Build on a variety of resources to learn words through multiple exposures

Increasing the students' awareness of words and how they can learn them is the first step involved in vocabulary instruction in mathematics. Obviously, mathematics teachers have an enormous task before them: they must teach a large number of complex and wholly unfamiliar topics to students that often involve unfamiliar vocabulary. Mathematics learning is vital to the welfare of the world in terms of protecting the economy, managing finance, and understanding the chemistry of living things. The first step in improving reading comprehension skills in students in mathematics is to develop their vocabularies.

## Selecting Vocabulary to Teach

It is not enough to know that word knowledge is complex; teachers must also know how and when to select the vocabulary for explicit instruction in the classroom.

The students themselves are the best resources for determining the words that they know and do not know. Mathematics teachers can create a list of vocabulary words about a particular topic or for a selected reading assignment and ask the students to indicate their level of understanding for each word. For example, if the reading is about linear functions, the list might include *slope*, *x-axis*, *y-axis*, *constant*, *x-intercept*, and *y-intercept*. If students indicate that they do not recognize any of the terms, the teacher can better plan the unit to address this issue. This task can make assessing student knowledge of specific words efficient and effective.

Ryder and Graves (2003) also suggest that students skim the reading material in advance and create their own list of words that are difficult, are particularly essential, or may need more clarification in class for successful comprehension of the reading material. This is a task that can be completed in cooperative groups.

# Developing Vocabulary in Mathematics *(cont.)*

## Selecting Vocabulary to Teach *(cont.)*

The following guidelines from Ryder and Graves (2003) will help teachers select vocabulary words to teach in class.

1. The words are important to the understanding of the reading selection.

2. The students cannot use context or their structural knowledge to determine the general meaning. If students can glean the meaning of the word because they recognize the root or compound parts, it is not always necessary to teach the word.

3. The words are useful outside of the assigned reading selection. If students are likely to encounter the word in another reading task outside of class, it is a valuable word to teach.

When selecting vocabulary for instruction, be sure to account for the incidental words that come up in class discussions and question-answer sessions. For example, when the word *distance* comes up in a class discussion, take the time to explain it, as it is a word that will be used across disciplines. Addressing vocabulary questions as they arise promotes word consciousness. Also, it is important to note that most teachers assign too many vocabulary words at one time.

> Teach no more than ten new words to middle and high school students, no more than five to upper-grade students, and only one or two to primary-grade students for each reading selection (chapter, article, or lesson).

## Promoting Word Consciousness

Students who are word conscious know the power of words, and they know a lot about words and how to use them. Word-conscious students enjoy using words cleverly, in precise and effective ways. They are interested in words in general, like to play with language, and pay close attention to the ways in which others use words. Word consciousness is directly connected to vocabulary development, which in turn helps students comprehend reading materials more efficiently and effectively. Developing word consciousness in mathematics helps students become critical thinkers and strategic readers.

Promoting curiosity and interest in words takes effort on the part of the mathematics teacher. Ryder and Graves (2003) suggest the following ways to promote word consciousness:

- Include precise, novel, and perhaps colorful words when talking with students.

- Point out particularly adept word choices in the material students are reading.

- Compliment students when they make adroit word choices in their speech or writing.

- Discuss connotations and other subtleties of words, particularly value-laden ones.

- Engage students in empirical inquiries about words.

# Vocabulary Strategies to Promote Word Consciousness in Mathematics

## Word Wall

### Background Information

A Word Wall is a bulletin board display of key vocabulary or concept words. Word Walls are a common component of elementary classrooms because they are a great way to expose students to new words. However, Word Walls can be just as effective in middle school. Middle-school teachers or teachers who work with multiple student groups throughout the day may use a flip chart as a Word Wall so that words can be added and removed as needed for each individual class. It is a great idea to involve students in the creation of Word Walls, so they feel a sense of ownership and pride in the wall. Exposing the students repeatedly to the words on a larger scale helps imprint the words in their long-term memories.

### Grade Levels/Standards Addressed

Grades 1–2 (Standard 5.6)
Grades 3–5 (Standard 5.7)
Grades 6–8 (Standard 5.3)

### Preparation

Using strips of tagboard or brightly colored construction paper, have students neatly print the words by hand. The strips should be large enough for the print to be easily read from a distance. Illustrations may be included. Always place the words on a specific wall area so that students will know to refer to this site for the current vocabulary. When "new" terms are introduced, move the "old" words to a different location where they are still accessible. Have students periodically "read the wall" for review. Encourage the use of the Word Wall as a reference for correct spelling. Advocate the application of new and old vocabulary in class discussions and assignments.

### Activity

Prior to reading about a specific mathematics topic, create a bulletin board display that includes all of the words about the topic. For example, if students are studying various properties, include associative property $[(a + b) + c = a + (b + c)]$, commutative property $[(a + b) = (b + a)]$, and distributive property $[a(b + c) = ab + ac]$. Have the students illustrate the properties using numbers and/or variables. The students can also group the concepts together on the bulletin board.

### Differentiation

This strategy is particularly helpful for ELLs because it exposes them to the target terms, and they can easily refer to the words any time. Include photos, illustrations, or examples for each word and provide students with take-home versions of the words on the board so that they can refer to them outside the classroom. Encourage gifted students to use more challenging words and explain how they relate to one another. Give students reading below grade level copies of the words from the Word Wall for their notebooks and repeatedly prompt them to refer to the wall or their lists. It may help to provide additional words on the list to help stimulate their thinking.

# Vocabulary Strategies to Promote Word Consciousness in Mathematics (cont.)

## Word Wall (cont.)

**Grades 1–2 Example**

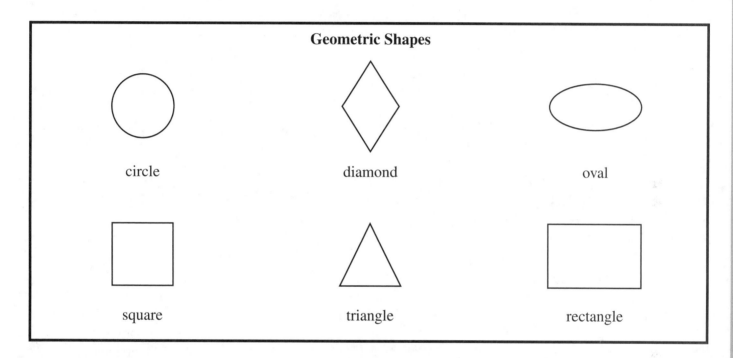

**Grades 3–5 Example**

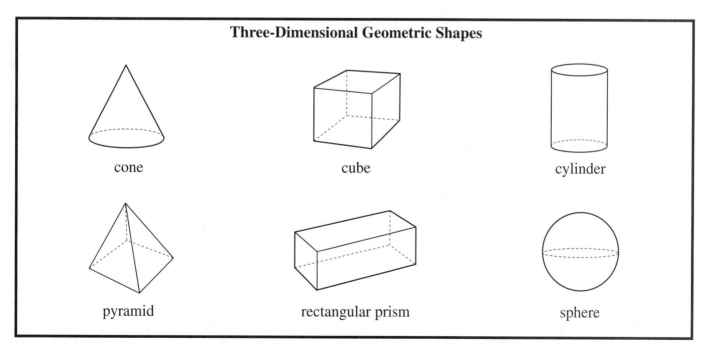

# Vocabulary Strategies to Promote
# Word Consciousness in Mathematics (cont.)

## Word Wall (cont.)

**Grades 6–8 Example**

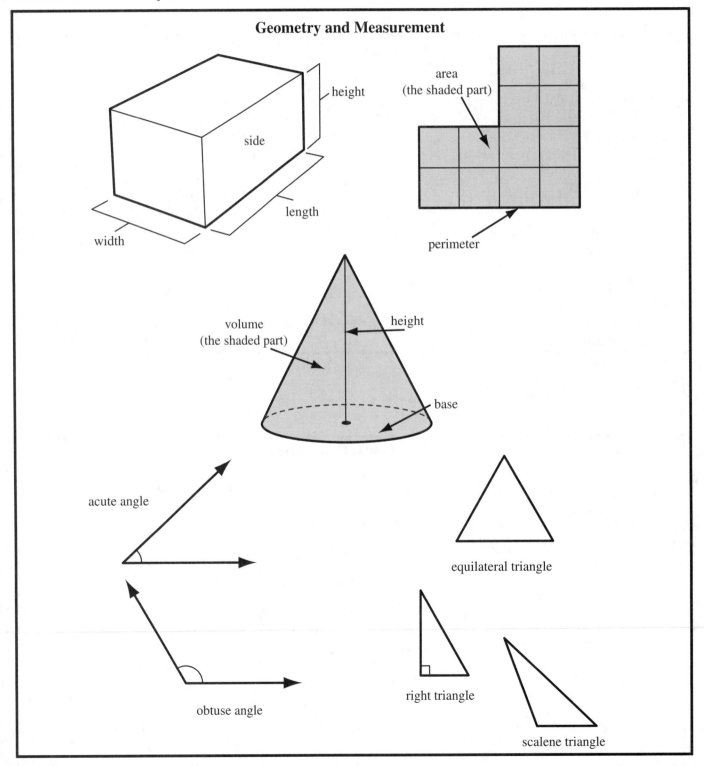

**Geometry and Measurement**

height

side

length

width

area
(the shaded part)

perimeter

volume
(the shaded part)

height

base

acute angle

obtuse angle

equilateral triangle

right triangle

scalene triangle

# Vocabulary Strategies to Promote
# Word Consciousness in Mathematics *(cont.)*

## Knowledge Rating Scale

### Background Information

The Knowledge Rating Scale (Blachowicz 1986, as cited by Lenski, Wham, and Johns 1999) is a vocabulary activity that allows students to rate their knowledge of target content words. It can also be used to assess the students' prior knowledge on a concept. When creating the list, the mathematics teacher should select only words that are essential to understanding the necessary concepts for the unit. In addition, it is helpful if the words have relevance outside of class. Teachers should give the students the survey to complete independently at the beginning of a lesson or unit. The list is a very useful assessment tool to evaluate the students' prior knowledge of mathematics vocabulary terms and concepts. After evaluating the responses on the Knowledge Rating Scale, teachers can determine the level of depth needed when teaching the various concepts represented by the words. The Knowledge Rating Scale is also an excellent review tool for students to use at any point in the lesson or unit.

### Grade Levels/Standards Addressed

Grades 3–5 (Standards 5.3, 5.5)
Grades 6–8 (Standards 5.2, 5.3)

### Activity

Before beginning a unit or lesson, scan the mathematics material that students will be reading. Locate ten words that are essential to understanding the main concepts. Place the words on the Knowledge Rating Scale form (page 31), and distribute the survey to the students. Ask students to complete the form independently. Before collecting the surveys, teachers can review each term with the students and ask them for a show of hands for each rating. Allowing for class discussion about the words will allow the students to make connections between the words and ideas that are shared.

### Differentiation

Include words or concepts that are generally or widely known to help ELLs make stronger connections to their previous knowledge. Group words on the list in a meaningful way. For example, the terms *numerator* and *denominator* could be listed together to help foster associations with concepts. Add additional words to the list for gifted students to help assess their content knowledge and plan accordingly. Be sure to read aloud all of the words on the list prior to asking students reading below grade level to rate them. Also, take notes and/or draw on the board to reinforce new vocabulary and concepts for them during the discussion of the survey.

# Vocabulary Strategies to Promote
# Word Consciousness in Mathematics (cont.)

## Knowledge Rating Scale (cont.)

**Grades 3–5 Example**

| Word | Know It Well | Have Heard/Seen It | No Clue |
|---|---|---|---|
| 1. inch | X | | |
| 2. foot | X | | |
| 3. yard | X | | |
| 4. mile | | | X |
| 5. meter | X | | |
| 6. millimeter | | | X |
| 7. centimeter | | | X |
| 8. kilometer | | | X |
| 9. unit | | | X |
| 10. perimeter | | X | |

**Grades 6–8 Example**

| Word | Know It Well | Have Heard/Seen It | No Clue |
|---|---|---|---|
| 1. ratio | | | X |
| 2. rate | X | | |
| 3. round | X | | |
| 4. estimate | X | | |
| 5. percentage | X | | |
| 6. multiple | X | | |
| 7. factor | | X | |
| 8. composite | | | X |
| 9. prime number | | | X |
| 10. integer | | X | |

**Name:** _____

# Knowledge Rating Scale

| Word | Know It Well | Have Heard/ Seen It | No Clue | Definition |
|---|---|---|---|---|
| 1. | | | | |
| 2. | | | | |
| 3. | | | | |
| 4. | | | | |
| 5. | | | | |
| 6. | | | | |
| 7. | | | | |
| 8. | | | | |
| 9. | | | | |
| 10. | | | | |

# Vocabulary Strategies to Promote Word Consciousness in Mathematics *(cont.)*

## Rating Vocabulary

## Background Information

Rating Vocabulary is an activity that allows students to rate their knowledge of target vocabulary words at specific points during the reading process. The teacher generates a list of key mathematics terms for the lesson and asks the students to evaluate their understanding of each term before reading, after reading, and after discussing the words. Students are given a Rating Vocabulary sheet at the beginning of a lesson or unit. The activity encourages students to think metacognitively about their understanding of each word and the related concepts. It also promotes the independent acquisition of new vocabulary.

### Grade Levels/Standards Addressed

Grades 3–5 (Standards 5.3, 5.5)
Grades 6–8 (Standards 5.2, 5.3, 5.4)

## Activity

Prior to assigning a reading selection, choose the most essential words in the lesson or unit. Create a Rating Vocabulary sheet (page 34) with the selected words. Give the students a copy of the Rating Vocabulary sheet and explain that they will be thinking about their understanding of particular words at three different points: before reading, after reading, and after discussing the words with the class. Explain the rating values: (+) indicates students know the word; (–) indicates students do not know the word; and (?) indicates students are not sure of the meaning of the word.

Ask students to read the words silently and rate the words in the Before Reading column on their sheets. After students have read the selected text, ask them to rate the words again in the After Reading column. Place students in small cooperative groups, or hold a class discussion in which students share which words they knew before reading, which words they were able to figure out during reading, and what they think the words mean. Clarify any words they still do not know. Have students complete the After Discussion column of the sheet. As a class, discuss which strategies the students used to determine the meaning of unknown words.

## Differentiation

Recite the words on the list or have classmates recite them to make sure ELLs understand the target words. Include known forms of the target words—like *multiply* for *multiplication*—because they will be better able to build on their prior knowledge. Select more challenging words for the same concepts for gifted students and encourage their independent exploration of their meanings. Students reading below grade level may get discouraged during the before-reading stage if they do not recognize any of the words, so select two or three words that they are sure to know to build their confidence and motivation.

# Vocabulary Strategies to Promote Word Consciousness in Mathematics *(cont.)*

## Rating Vocabulary *(cont.)*

### Grades 3–5 Example

**Directions:** Fill out each column at three different stages of reading a section of your textbook: before you read, after you read, and after the discussion. Use the following key to indicate your understanding of the word: (+) I know the word; (–) I do not know the word; and (?) I am not sure of the meaning of the word.

| Word | Before Reading | After Reading | After Discussion |
|------|:---:|:---:|:---:|
| 1. sum | + | + | + |
| 2. difference | – | + | + |
| 3. more than | – | – | + |
| 4. less than | – | + | + |
| 5. equal to | + | + | + |
| 6. product | + | + | + |
| 7. one-digit | – | – | + |
| 8. two-digit | + | + | + |
| 9. three-digit | – | + | + |
| 10. place value | – | – | + |

### Grades 6–8 Example

**Directions:** Fill out each column at three different stages of reading a section of your textbook: before you read, after you read, and after the discussion. Use the following key to indicate your understanding of the word: (+) I know the word; (–) I do not know the word; and (?) I am not sure of the meaning of the word.

| Word | Before Reading | After Reading | After Discussion |
|------|:---:|:---:|:---:|
| 1. scientific notation | + | + | + |
| 2. rational number | + | + | + |
| 3. irrational number | ? | + | + |
| 4. whole number | – | ? | + |
| 5. exponent | + | + | + |
| 6. positive power | – | – | + |
| 7. negative power | – | – | + |
| 8. inverse | + | + | + |
| 9. square root | – | ? | + |
| 10. absolute value | – | ? | + |

# Rating Vocabulary

**Directions:** Fill out each column at three different stages of reading a section of your textbook: before you read, after you read, and after the discussion.  Use the following key to indicate your understanding of the word: (+) I know the word; (–) I do not know the word; and (?) I am not sure of the meaning of the word.

| Word | Before Reading | After Reading | After Discussion |
|---|---|---|---|
| 1. | | | |
| 2. | | | |
| 3. | | | |
| 4. | | | |
| 5. | | | |
| 6. | | | |
| 7. | | | |
| 8. | | | |
| 9. | | | |
| 10. | | | |

# Vocabulary Strategies for the Analysis of Word Parts in Mathematics

## The Analysis of Word Parts in Mathematics

Breaking down and examining word parts—prefixes, suffixes, base words, blends, digraphs, and Greek and Latin roots—is another approach to teaching vocabulary that can help students learn the thousands of words they need to study mathematics. There is increasing evidence that it helps to teach students the major word chunks in English (Ryder and Graves 2003; Pressley 2000). *Morphology* is the ability to use word structures to make meaning of new vocabulary. Explicit instruction that teaches students to use their prior knowledge to make sense of root words, suffixes, prefixes, and other word parts builds confidence in understanding words and ultimately increases reading comprehension skills. Simply put, when students recognize Greek and Latin roots and other word parts in unfamiliar words, they are better able to make accurate guesses at the definitions, and therefore better understand what they are reading in mathematics.

Before teachers do direct instruction on word parts in mathematics, it is best to assess students' understanding of what they already know about word parts. Ryder and Graves (2003) suggest a few activities to determine what students know about prefixes and suffixes. Give the students a list of words that have various prefixes. Have the students remove the prefixes from the words, and then define the prefixes. Then, give the students a list of words that have a variety of suffixes. Have them remove the suffixes from the words and define the suffixes.

| Words with Prefixes | Prefix | Prefix Definition |
|---|---|---|
| proportion | pro- | forward, in favor of |
| polygon | poly- | many |
| multiply | multi- | many, much |
| symmetry | sym- | with, together |
| kilometer | kilo- | thousand |
| equilateral | equi- | equal |
| triangle | tri- | three |

| Words with Suffixes | Suffix | Suffix Definition |
|---|---|---|
| average | -age | belongs to |
| equilateral | -al | relating to |
| negative | -ive | like |
| different | -ent | to form |
| supplementary | -ary | relating to, like |
| multiplication | -tion | being the result of |
| divisor | -or | thing that |

# Vocabulary Strategies for the Analysis of Word Parts in Mathematics *(cont.)*

## The Analysis of Word Parts in Mathematics *(cont.)*

Ask any adult who studied Latin or Greek in grade or high school, and that adult will extol the virtues of teaching Latin and Greek to all students. This is because most modern English words originated from these languages. This is particularly important in mathematics, where students encounter a large number of Greek- and Latin-based words. Teachers can do a similar activity with common Greek and Latin root words. Make a list of words that contain Greek or Latin roots, and ask students to identify and define the root. Teachers can also group words with common roots together and ask students to determine what the root means.

Ryder and Graves (2003) also suggest that teachers use direct instruction to teach common Greek and Latin roots as well as prefixes and suffixes. Mathematics teachers can teach the word parts that are most useful in mathematics, that appear most frequently in the reading material, and that will appear in contexts outside mathematics class. It is important to provide students with a resource to locate the definitions of word parts as they read independently. Mathematics teachers should create bulletin boards of common roots, prefixes, and suffixes with examples of words that include the word parts and provide students with comprehensive lists to keep in their notebooks for easy reference. See pages 46–47 for a list of Greek and Latin roots.

| Words with Root | Root Word/Meaning |
|---|---|
| cent, century, centimeter, percent, percentage | cent = one hundred |
| circle, circumference, circumscribe, circular | circ, circum = around |
| centimeter, kilometer, metric | meter, metr = measure |
| probable, probability, probabilities | prob = to prove, test |
| intersect, intersecting, bisect | sect = cut |

# Vocabulary Strategies for the Analysis of Word Parts in Mathematics *(cont.)*

## Root Word Tree

## Background Information

The Root Word Tree is a graphic organizer that allows students to examine a single vocabulary word for its different word parts. When using the graphic organizer, students locate an unknown word, write it at the base of the tree, and break apart the word into recognizable chunks to help them decipher its meaning. They also can write down additional words that are associated with the word parts to help them remember the definition.

### Grade Levels/Standards Addressed

Grades 1–2 (Standard 5.4)
Grades 3–5 (Standard 5.4)

## Activity

The reading selection should contain some words that are unknown to the students. Instruct the students to locate an unknown word that is essential to their understanding of the passage. Tell them to write the word in the box at the base of the tree on the Root Word Tree graphic organizer (page 39). Next, have students break up the word and place the word parts on the large limbs of the tree. Ask students to write down other words with those same word parts on the branches of the tree. After having students work independently or in small groups, lead the whole class in a discussion and review session in which the students present and share their work.

## Differentiation

ELLs should have the target vocabulary word selected for them and written in the box. They will benefit from working in small heterogeneous groups to lower their anxiety levels and to practice sharing ideas in a small-group setting prior to sharing with the entire class. ELLs may also need a dictionary as a reference tool. Gifted students should be encouraged to use reference tools to examine the words more closely and research the etymology of the words and the meaning of the word parts. Students reading below grade level will benefit from teacher scaffolding. Write some of the word parts or associated words on the tree to help students understand the process.

# Vocabulary Strategies for the Analysis of Word Parts in Mathematics (cont.)

## Root Word Tree (cont.)

### Grades 1–2 Example

**Directions:** Write the unknown word in the box at the base of the tree. Break up the word into parts, and write the parts on the limbs. Think of other words that include the parts, and write those on the branches.

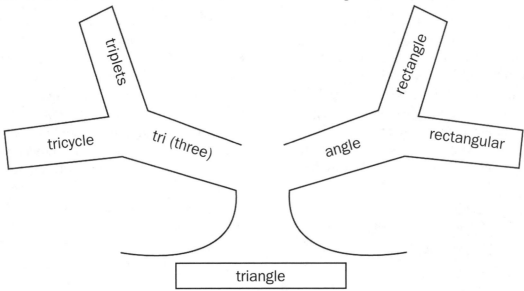

### Grades 3–5 Example

**Directions:** Write the unknown word in the box at the base of the tree. Break up the word into parts, and write the parts on the limbs. Think of other words that include the parts, and write those on the branches.

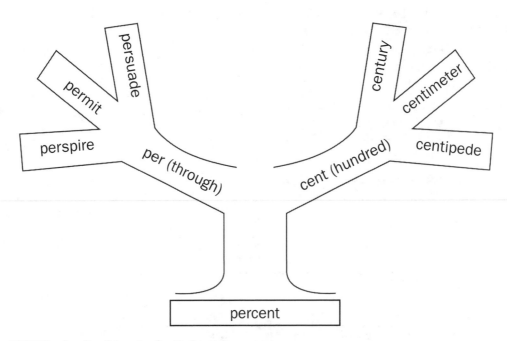

**Name:** _____

# Root Word Tree

**Directions:** Write the unknown word in the box at the base of the tree. Break up the word into parts, and write the parts on the limbs. Think of other words that include the parts, and write those on the branches.

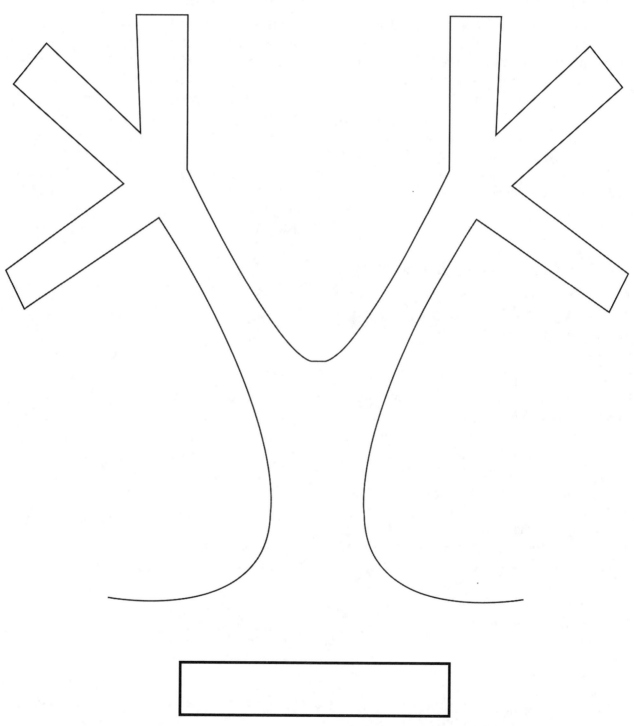

# Vocabulary Strategies for the Analysis of Word Parts in Mathematics *(cont.)*

## Root Word Map

## Background Information

The Root Word Map is a conceptual tool that helps students make word associations with the roots of words and promotes the long-term memory's acquisition of new words. Students should be encouraged to use the dictionary for some, but not all, vocabulary activities. Besides learning how to spell and pronounce words, the dictionary provides the history of the word and its roots. After students identify the root of a particular word, they should use the dictionary to locate additional words that share the same root.

### Grade Levels/Standards Addressed

Grades 3–5 (Standards 5.4, 5.6)
Grades 6–8 (Standard 5.2)

## Activity

Instruct students to find the root of a vocabulary word from their reading. Allow students to use dictionaries to identify the root word, its etymology, and other words that use the same root. Then have students use the Root Word Map (page 42) to demonstrate how the words are related in meaning. Instruct them to place the root in the main box of the graphic organizer. Give students dictionaries to locate other words that have the same root and place those on the graphic organizer. When students are finished, ask them to explain how the words in their map are related. Hold a class discussion about other organizational possibilities.

## Differentiation

It will help ELLs to have some of the words written on the graphic organizer for them so that they can concentrate on understanding the relationships among the new words. Place these students in small heterogeneous groups that include strong readers and students reading below grade level to help them understand the subtle differences between the different words. Gifted students should be encouraged to articulate and explain the relationships among all of the words. To challenge gifted students, ask them to reorganize the words using a different strategy.

# Vocabulary Strategies for the Analysis of Word Parts in Mathematics *(cont.)*

## Root Word Map *(cont.)*

### Grades 3–5 Example

**Directions:** Place the root of the vocabulary word in the first box. Look in the dictionary or use the Internet to locate words that have the same root. Determine how the words are related to each other, and place them in the boxes below.

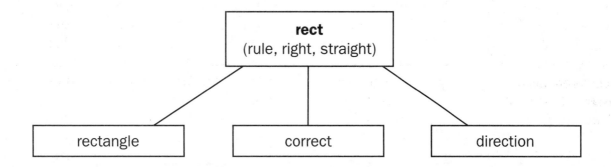

### Grades 6–8 Example

**Directions:** Place the root of the vocabulary word in the first box. Look in the dictionary or use the Internet to locate words that have the same root. Determine how the words are related to each other, and place them in the boxes below.

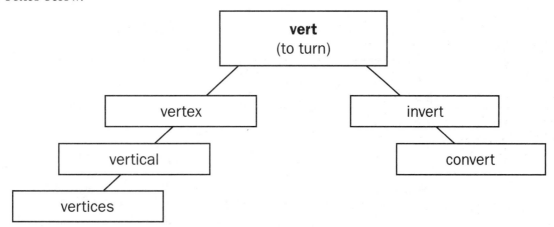

**Name:** _____

# Root Word Map

**Directions:** Write the root of the vocabulary word in the first box. Look in the dictionary or use the Internet to locate words that have the same root. Determine how the words are related to each other, and write them in the boxes below.

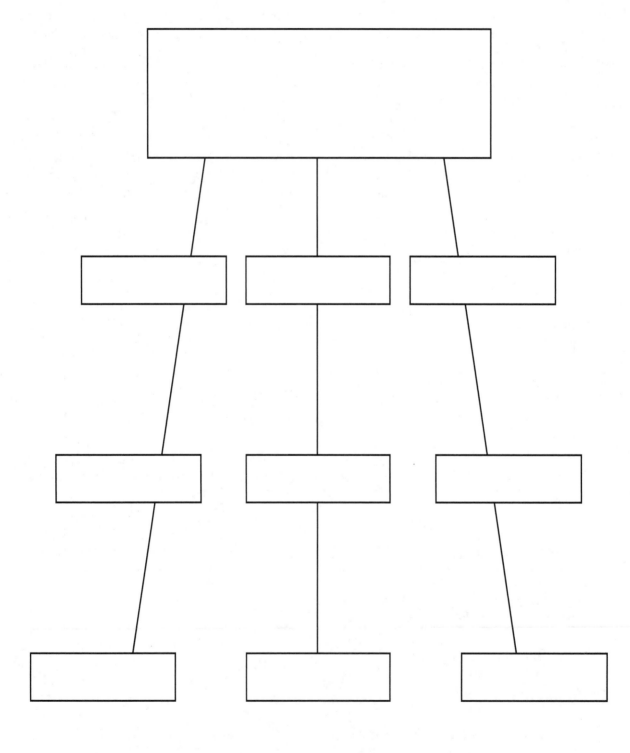

 #50055—*Reading Strategies for Mathematics*

# Vocabulary Strategies for the Analysis of Word Parts in Mathematics (cont.)

## Roots/Prefixes/Suffixes Chart

### Background Information

The Roots/Prefixes/Suffixes Chart helps students track unknown words they encounter while reading independently. The chart specifically asks students to write down unknown words, and any roots, prefixes, and suffixes that may be a part of the word and to guess the word's definition. When students in mathematics examine unknown words in this way, they can better learn the meanings of the different word parts, which helps them decode unknown words as they read. Furthermore, allowing students to guess the definition enables them to personalize their learning (Nagy and Scott 2000). Word part analysis can be introduced informally, beginning in kindergarten when students learn the orthographic patterns of many words. For example, kindergartners, although they may not be able to explain it, can easily understand that number words that end in -*th* and -*eth* are ordinal numbers (*fifth*, *sixth*, *twelfth*). As students progress through the upper grades, they will encounter hundreds of words that have roots, prefixes, and suffixes within them, perhaps more in mathematics than in any other subject area. In grades 3–5, students should examine no more than three words per reading selection. In grades 6–8, students should examine no more than five words per reading selection.

### Grade Levels/Standards Addressed

Grades 3–5 (Standard 5.4)
Grades 6–8 (Standard 5.2)

### Activity

Distribute copies of the Roots/Prefixes/Suffixes Chart (page 45) to the students prior to beginning a reading selection from the mathematics textbook, a trade book, or an article. Ask students to pay attention to words they do not know as they read. Have students work independently or in pairs to record the unknown words. Ask them to look up the roots, prefixes, and suffixes and record these as well. Encourage the students to guess the meaning of the unknown word based on the word parts' definitions. When the students have completed the sheet, meet as a class to discuss the unknown words, as well as what the students think they mean. Encourage students to discuss how they arrived at their guesses. Review the true definitions of the words and compare and contrast them to their guesses.

### Differentiation

ELLs will benefit from working with a partner during this activity. Cooperative learning lowers the anxiety levels of ELLs and promotes collaboration. Encourage gifted students to locate additional words that include the same roots, prefixes, and suffixes and write them on the back of their charts so that they can later share with the whole group. Students reading below grade level may need the teacher to scaffold some of the graphic organizer as it will lower anxiety by making the task seem less overwhelming.

A valuable teaching resource for roots, prefixes, and suffixes is *The Reading Teacher's Book of Lists*, 5th ed., 2006, Jossey-Bass.

# Vocabulary Strategies for the Analysis of Word Parts in Mathematics *(cont.)*

## Roots/Prefixes/Suffixes Chart *(cont.)*

### Grades 3–5 Example

**Directions:** Identify the unknown words. Look up the roots, prefixes, and suffixes. Guess each word's definition.

| Unknown Word | Roots | Prefixes | Suffixes | Guess Definition |
|---|---|---|---|---|
| kilometer | meter (measure) | kilo- (thousand) | | thousand measures |
| percentage | cent (hundred) | per- (through) | -age (belongs to) | belongs to numbers through a hundred |
| perimeter | meter (measure) | peri- (around) | | to measure around |

### Grades 6–8 Example

**Directions:** Identify the unknown words. Look up the roots, prefixes, and suffixes. Guess each word's definition.

| Unknown Word | Roots | Prefixes | Suffixes | Guess Definition |
|---|---|---|---|---|
| intersecting | sect (cut) | inter- (between) | -ing (result of an activity) | result of cutting between |
| sequential | sequ (to follow) | | -ial (function of) | a function of the following |
| factor | fact (to make) | | -or (thing that) | thing that makes |

**Name:** _____

# Roots/Prefixes/Suffixes Chart

**Directions:** Identify the unknown words. Look up the roots, prefixes, and suffixes. Guess each word's definition.

| Unknown Word | Roots | Prefixes | Suffixes | Guess Definition |
|---|---|---|---|---|
|  |  |  |  |  |
|  |  |  |  |  |
|  |  |  |  |  |
|  |  |  |  |  |
|  |  |  |  |  |

# Vocabulary Strategies for the Analysis of Word Parts in Mathematics *(cont.)*

## Greek and Latin Roots

| Root | Meaning | Examples |
|------|---------|----------|
| ac, acr (L) | sharp | acute, accuracy, acceleration |
| ced, cess, cede (L) | to yield, to go | antecedent, process, precede |
| cent (L) | one hundred | century, centimeter, percent |
| cept, capt, cap, ceive (L) | to take, hold, grasp | intercept, caption, perceive |
| cert (L) | sure, to trust | certain |
| circ, circum (L) | around | circle, circular, circumference |
| cline (L) | lean | incline, decline |
| cont (L) | to join, unite | continuous, continuously |
| crit, cris (L) | separate, discern, judge | criteria |
| equ (L) | equal, fair | equilateral, equivalent |
| fac, fic, fec, fect, fact (L) | to make, to do | factor, factorization, affect |
| famil (L) | family | fact family |
| fer, fero, latus (L) | to carry, bear, bring | differ, difference, infer, translate |
| fin (L) | to end | infinite, finite |
| form (L) | shape, form | inform, formula, formulate |
| fract (L) | break | fraction |
| graph, gram (G) | write, draw, describe, record | graphing, graphic, kilogram |
| lat (L) | lateral, side, wide | equilateral |
| log (G) | idea, word, speech, reason | logarithm, logarithmical, logistic |
| med, medi (L) | middle | median |
| men, min, mon (L) | to think, remind, advise, warn | minimize, minimum |
| ment (L) | mind | mental math |
| meter, metri (G) | measure | kilometer, millimeter, metric |
| null, nihil, nil (L) | nothing, void | null set |
| ord, ordin (L) | order | order, ordinal, ordered |
| pend, pond, pens (L) | to weigh, pay, consider | perpendicular |
| plur, plus (L) | more | plus sign, plural |
| pos, posit, pon (L) | to place, put | positive, position |
| prim, prin (L) | first | principle, primary, prime |
| prob (L) | to prove, test | probable, problem, probability |
| rect, reg, rig, reign (L) | rule, right, straight | rectangle, rectangular, correct |
| script (L) | to write | subscript, superscript |
| sect (L) | cut | intersect, bisect, intersecting |
| sequ, seque, sequi (L) | to follow | sequence, sequential |
| simil, simul (L) | together, likeness, pretense | similar, simultaneous |
| tang, tact, ting (L) | to touch | tangent, contact, contingent |
| term (L) | end, limit, boundary | interminable, terminate |
| vert (L) | to turn | vertex, vertical, vertices, invert |

#50055—*Reading Strategies for Mathematics*   © *Shell Education*

# Vocabulary Strategies for the Analysis of Word Parts in Mathematics *(cont.)*

## Greek and Latin Prefixes

| Prefix | Meaning | Examples |
|---|---|---|
| bi (L) | two | binary, binomial |
| co, con, com (L) | together, with | congruent, concave |
| contra, contro (L) | against | contradictory, contrapositive |
| de (L) | from, away, off | degree, denominator |
| deca, dec, deka (G) | ten | decagon, decimeter |
| dia (G) | through, across | diamond, diameter |
| dis, dif (L) | apart, away, not, to deprive | discriminant, difference |
| e, ex, ec (L) | out, beyond, from, out of | expanded, expression |
| hemi (G) | half | hemisphere |
| hepta, hept (G) | seven | heptagon |
| hexa, hex (G) | six | hexagon |
| hypo, hyp (G) | under, less than | hypotenuse |
| in, ir, im, il (L) | not, without | inverse |
| inter (L) | between | intersect, intersecting |
| iso (G) | equal | isosceles |
| kilo (G) | thousand | kilogram, kilometer |
| mono (G) | one | monomial |
| multi (L) | many, much | multi-digit, multiplication, multiply |
| nona, non (L) | nine | nonagon |
| o, ob, oc, of, op (L) | against, toward | obtuse |
| oct, octa, octo (G) | eight | octagon |
| para (L) | beside, beyond | parallel, parallelogram |
| penta (G) | five | pentagon |
| per (L) | through | percent, percentage |
| peri (G) | around, about | perimeter, periodic |
| pro (L) | before, forward, forth | product, proportion |
| poly (G) | many | polygon, polynomial |
| quad, quatr (L) | four | quadrilateral, quadrangle |
| re (L) | again, anew, back | reduce, reciprocal |
| semi (L) | half | semicircle |
| sub (L) | under, below, up from below | subtract, subtraction |
| syn, sym, syl (G) | together, with | symbol |
| trans (L) | over, across | transpose |
| tri (L) | three | triangle |
| uni (L) | one | uniform |

Adapted from Edward Bernard Fry, Jacqueline E. Kress, and Dona Lee Fountoukidis, *The Reading Teacher's Book of Lists,* 4th ed. *[San Francisco: Jossey-Bass, 2000], 106–111.*

# Activating Knowledge Through Vocabulary Development in Mathematics

## Building Vocabulary Connections

Effective vocabulary instruction in mathematics involves helping students relate new vocabulary words to what they already know. By helping students make strong connections between their prior knowledge on a topic and new words and concepts in mathematics, teachers can greatly increase the long-term retention of mathematics vocabulary. Furthermore, relating new words to previous experiences leads to improved reading comprehension (Lenski, Wham, and Johns 1999).

Associating an experience or a concept with a word is fundamental to the reading process, and word knowledge is absolutely necessary when learning how to comprehend texts efficiently. Students come to school and to each classroom with a variety of experiences and knowledge. They arrive with finite vocabulary to describe the world around them and their own experiences. It is through new experiences and interactions with reading materials, classmates, and the teacher that they articulate their experiences and new understandings, as well as expand the meaning of the words they use.

## Personalizing Word Learning

The most important aspect of activating knowledge through vocabulary instruction is to personalize what is learned for the students. Making this personal connection greatly enhances the students' ability to retain the meaning of new mathematics vocabulary words so that they can recognize them in print and use them in their own speech and writing. Research in vocabulary instruction supports the active engagement of students in making connections between and among words (Blachowicz and Fisher 2000). Students should be encouraged to articulate their personal understanding of words as they encounter them, to select what words they will study and learn, and to determine which strategies to use when they become more independent at comprehending reading material.

# Vocabulary Strategies to Activate Knowledge in Mathematics

## Concept of Definition Map

### Background Information

The Concept of Definition Map (Schwartz and Raphael 1985) is a graphic organizer used to teach the definitions of the most essential vocabulary terms. These terms should represent important concepts in the reading material. The Concept of Definition Map encourages students to learn more than just the dictionary definition of key terms. It helps them learn the subtleties and nuances of particular words, which are reinforced by the visual organization of the information in a graphic organizer. Included in the Concept of Definition Map are the categories or classes for the term (What is it?), the properties or characteristics of the term (What are some things you know about it?), comparison terms (What is it like?), and illustrations or examples (What does it look like?). The analogies that students create promote long-term memory by personalizing the association of the concept.

### Grade Levels/Standards Addressed

Grades 1–2 (Standard 5.1)
Grades 3–5 (Standards 5.6, 5.7)
Grades 6–8 (Standard 5.3)

### Activity

Prior to assigning a reading selection, choose a word that is key to comprehending the text. Write the term on the board and at the center of the Concept of Definition Map (page 52). Guide the students in adding to the map by asking them the following questions:

- What is it?
- What are some things you know about it?
- What is it like?
- What is an example of it?

Encourage students to then read the text and add information to the map. Ask students in grades 6–8 to think of an original analogy to explain what the concept is like. After completing the map, ask the students to use their maps as guidelines to write a definition of the concept. Meet as a class to discuss student answers, and then write examples of good definitions on the board as models for the students.

### Differentiation

ELLs will benefit from working with a partner during this activity. Cooperative learning lowers the anxiety levels of ELL students and promotes collaboration. Encourage gifted students to complete further research by collecting the definitions and examples from various resources, not just the textbook, and combining them into a definition that is a synthesis of what they have learned. Students reading below grade level will benefit from the teacher filling out a section of the graphic organizer prior to distributing them to the students. This will help the students orient themselves with concepts and ideas and lower their anxiety.

# Vocabulary Strategies to Activate Knowledge in Mathematics *(cont.)*

## Concept of Definition Map *(cont.)*

### Grades 1–2 Example

**Directions:** Fill out the different categories for the selected word. Use a dictionary or a thesaurus if necessary.

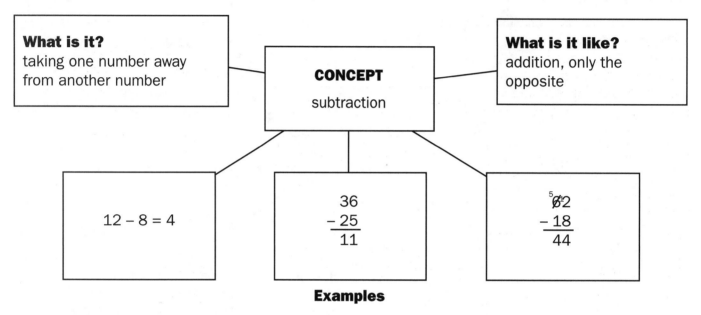

**What is it?**
taking one number away from another number

**CONCEPT**
subtraction

**What is it like?**
addition, only the opposite

$12 - 8 = 4$

$$\begin{array}{r} 36 \\ -\ 25 \\ \hline 11 \end{array}$$

$$\begin{array}{r} ^{5}\not{6}^{4}2 \\ -\ 18 \\ \hline 44 \end{array}$$

**Examples**

### Grades 3–5 Example

**Directions:** Fill out the different categories for the selected word. Use a dictionary or a thesaurus if necessary.

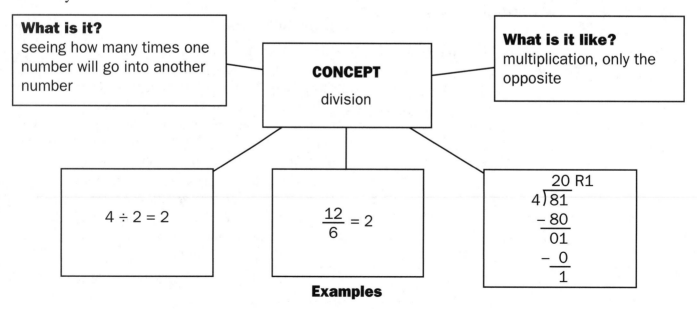

**What is it?**
seeing how many times one number will go into another number

**CONCEPT**
division

**What is it like?**
multiplication, only the opposite

$4 \div 2 = 2$

$$\frac{12}{6} = 2$$

$$\begin{array}{r} 20 \text{ R1} \\ 4\overline{)81} \\ -\ 80 \\ \hline 01 \\ -\ 0 \\ \hline 1 \end{array}$$

**Examples**

# Vocabulary Strategies to Activate Knowledge in Mathematics *(cont.)*

## Concept of Definition Map *(cont.)*

### Grades 6–8 Example

**Directions:** Fill out the different categories for the selected word.  Use a dictionary or a thesaurus if necessary.

---

**What is it?**
When given 2 equations with 2 different variables, solve one of the equations for a single variable, and substitute that entire value into the other equation.  Solve for the single variable.  Plug the answer into the first equation and solve for the second variable.

**CONCEPT**
substitution method for systems of equations

**What is it like?**
Solving for a single variable, only with additional steps

---

**Examples**

$x = y + 1$
$3x = y + 9$

$3x = y + 9$
$3(y + 1) = y + 9$
$3y + 3 = y + 9$
$3y - y + 3 = y - y + 9$
$2y + 3 = 9$
$2y + 3 - 3 = 9 - 3$
$2y = 6$
$\dfrac{2y}{2} = \dfrac{6}{2}$
$y = 3$

$x = y + 1$
$x = 3 + 1$
$x = 4$

$(4, 3)$
$(x, y)$

---

$3x - y = 4$
$3x - 7y = 10$

$3x - y = 4$
$3x - 3x - y = 4 - 3x$
$-y = -3x + 4$
$-y(-1) = -3x + 4(-1)$
$y = 3x - 4$

$3x - 7y = 10$
$3x - 7(3x - 4) = 10$
$3x - 21x + 28 = 10$
$-18x + 28 = 10$
$-18x + 28 - 28 = 10 - 28$
$\dfrac{-18x}{-18} = \dfrac{-18}{-18}$
$x = 1$

$y = 3x - 4$
$y = 3(1) - 4$
$y = 3 - 4$
$y = -1$

$(1, -1)$
$(x, y)$

---

$x = y$
$8x = 40 - 2y$

$8x = 40 - 2y$
$8(y) = 40 - 2y$
$8y + 2y = 40 - 2y + 2y$
$\dfrac{10y}{10} = \dfrac{40}{10}$
$y = 4$

$x = y$
$x = (4)$
$x = 4$

$(4, 4)$
$(x, y)$

# Concept of Definition Map

**Directions:** Fill out the different categories for the selected word.  Use a dictionary or a thesaurus if necessary.

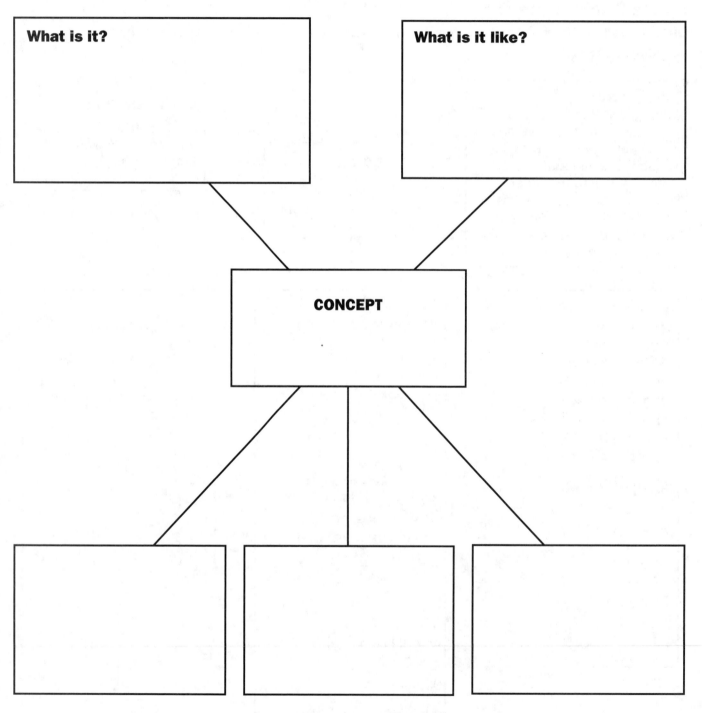

**What is it?**

**What is it like?**

**CONCEPT**

**Examples or Illustrations**

# Vocabulary Strategies to Activate Knowledge in Mathematics (cont.)

## Frayer Model

### Background Information

The Frayer Model (Frayer, Frederick, and Klausmeier 1969) is a strategy in which students use the graphic organizer as a means to better understand a concept and to distinguish that concept from others they may know or may be learning. The framework of the Frayer Model includes the concept word, the definition, the characteristics of the concept word, examples of the concept word, and non-examples of the concept word. It is important to include both examples and non-examples so that students are able to clarify what the concept word is and what it is not. The Frayer Model is especially useful for teaching mathematics vocabulary that describes complex concepts or vocabulary that describes mathematics concepts students may already know but cannot yet clearly define. Using the Frayer method takes a substantial amount of the teacher's and students' time and effort, but it provides students with a rich understanding of important concepts.

### Grade Levels/Standards Addressed

Grades 3–5 (Standard 5.6)
Grades 6–8 (Standard 5.3)

### Activity

Instruct the students to write down the word for a new concept they are learning on the Frayer Model graphic organizer (page 55). First, the teacher and the students must define the concept and list its attributes. The students may refer to their textbooks, using information in the margins or the glossary, or apposition in the text itself. Students may also consult other resources to find the definition or use the definition provided by the teacher.

Next, distinguish between the concept and similar concepts with which it might easily be confused. When doing this, help the students understand the concept in some depth. This can easily be accomplished through question-and-answer sessions during a short discussion. Also, provide the students with examples of the concept and explain why they are examples. Next, provide the students with non-examples of the concept and explain why they are non-examples. Discuss the examples and non-examples at length. Encourage students to generate their own examples and non-examples, and allow them to discuss their findings with the class. Once students are skilled at using the strategy, the entire class can work in pairs to complete a Frayer Model graphic organizer for different essential concepts and then present their findings to the class.

### Differentiation

Coach gifted students to model how to complete the organizer for the class. By placing a small group of two to three gifted students in the center of the room and allowing the class to observe their discussion and how they complete the organizer, ELLs will learn about the Frayer Model. Encourage the students who are modeling the technique to think aloud as they work through their ideas. Provide one-on-one instruction during the small group work for students reading below grade level and select a reasonable concept word.

# Vocabulary Strategies to Activate Knowledge in Mathematics *(cont.)*

## Frayer Model *(cont.)*

### Grades 3–5 Example

| Definition | Characteristics |
|---|---|
| Changing the number in the tens place to a simpler value based on the value in the ones place | If the number in the ones place is 5 or above, change the tens place up one and put a 0 in the ones place. If the number in the ones place is lower than 5, keep the number in the tens place the same and replace the number in the ones place with a 0. |
| **Examples**<br><br>47 becomes 50<br><br>624 becomes 620<br><br>1,562 becomes 1,560 | **Non-examples**<br><br>47 becomes 40 (rounding down instead of up)<br><br>624 becomes 600 (rounding to the nearest hundred instead of ten) |

**Word:** rounding (to the nearest ten)

### Grades 6–8 Example

| Definition | Characteristics |
|---|---|
| Applying a value that is outside a set of parentheses to all of the values inside the parentheses | Multiplication is used to apply the value outside the parentheses to the values inside the parentheses; value being distributed may be a single value or multiple values. |
| **Examples**<br><br>$4(x + y)$ becomes $4x + 4y$<br><br>$a(7b - 8a)$ becomes $7ab - 8a^2$ | **Non-examples**<br><br>$4(x + y)$ becomes $4xy$ (4 is not distributed individually to each term)<br><br>$a(7b - 8a)$ becomes $-a^2b$ (unlike terms $7b$ and $-8a$ combined) |

**Word:** distributive property

**Name:** _____

# Frayer Model

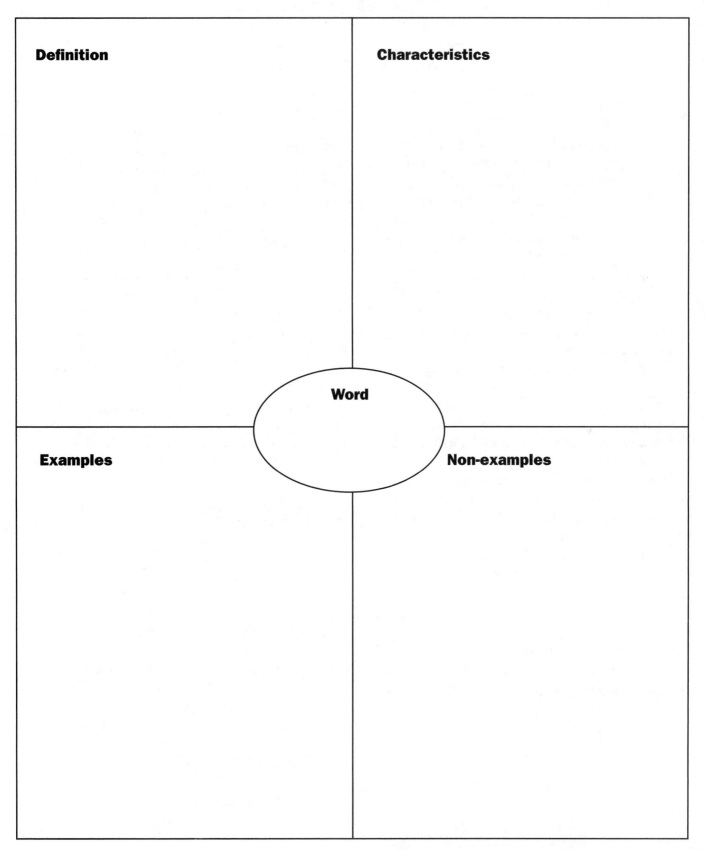

# Vocabulary Strategies to Activate Knowledge in Mathematics (cont.)

## Semantic Word Map

### Background Information

The Semantic Word Map allows students to explore their knowledge of a new word by creating a map using other related words or phrases similar in meaning to the new word. Semantic mapping (Heimlich and Pittelman 1986, as cited by Ryder and Graves 2003) is a form of intensive instruction that is appropriate for mathematics selections that have a single central concept and for students who have fairly substantial prior knowledge about the central concept. This vocabulary technique allows students to acquire a clearer definition of a mathematics concept by learning the connections among several related words. Emphasizing the interconnectedness of vocabulary words is an effective teaching strategy for vocabulary, according to Nagy and Scott (2000), because it taps into the way individuals store information in their brains. Furthermore, this strategy enhances vocabulary development by helping students link new information with previous experience. The activity can be used before reading to assess and build upon prior knowledge about a concept. The students can add additional information to their Semantic Word Maps after reading. The Semantic Word Map can also serve as a review tool at the end of a lesson or unit.

### Grade Levels/Standards Addressed

Grades 1–2 (Standard 7.4)
Grades 3–5 (Standard 7.6)
Grades 6–8 (Standard 7.4)

### Activity

Determine the central concept in a mathematics reading selection prior to assigning it to the students. It is important to think about important related ideas, events, characteristics, and examples to effectively prepare for a healthy discussion. After introducing the concept to students, ask them to brainstorm words relating to the concept. Record their ideas on the board. Expand the discussion around the words that suggest larger related categories, ideas, events, characteristics, and examples. Point out those words on the list that are likely to be most useful for organizing the main concept. Have students work independently to determine which words belong under the appropriate categories. Once students have completed their Semantic Word Maps (page 59), allow them to present them and explain their reasons for choosing each word for the appropriate category.

### Differentiation

ELL students will benefit from working in small, cooperative-learning groups for this activity. Working in groups will allow the students to discuss the reasons for their decisions, which encourages more active participation and engagement in the activity. Gifted students should be encouraged to explore larger related categories that interest them in more depth. If working in groups, gifted students can take the role of mediator in the decision-making process. Students below grade level should be encouraged to summarize the information on the graphic organizer for the entire class when the discussion is completed.

# Vocabulary Strategies to Activate Knowledge in Mathematics *(cont.)*

## Semantic Word Map *(cont.)*

### Grades 1–2 Example

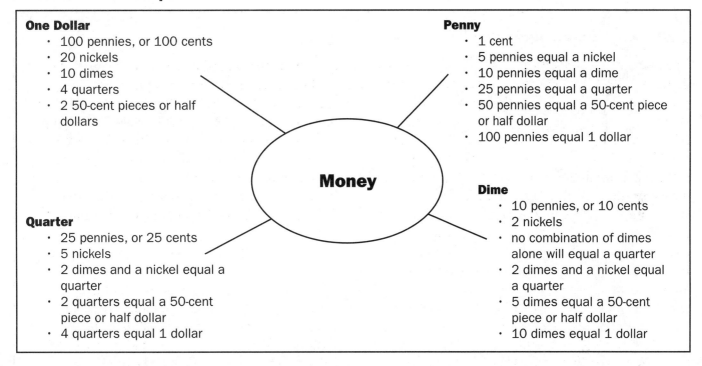

**One Dollar**
- 100 pennies, or 100 cents
- 20 nickels
- 10 dimes
- 4 quarters
- 2 50-cent pieces or half dollars

**Penny**
- 1 cent
- 5 pennies equal a nickel
- 10 pennies equal a dime
- 25 pennies equal a quarter
- 50 pennies equal a 50-cent piece or half dollar
- 100 pennies equal 1 dollar

**Money**

**Quarter**
- 25 pennies, or 25 cents
- 5 nickels
- 2 dimes and a nickel equal a quarter
- 2 quarters equal a 50-cent piece or half dollar
- 4 quarters equal 1 dollar

**Dime**
- 10 pennies, or 10 cents
- 2 nickels
- no combination of dimes alone will equal a quarter
- 2 dimes and a nickel equal a quarter
- 5 dimes equal a 50-cent piece or half dollar
- 10 dimes equal 1 dollar

### Grades 3–5 Example

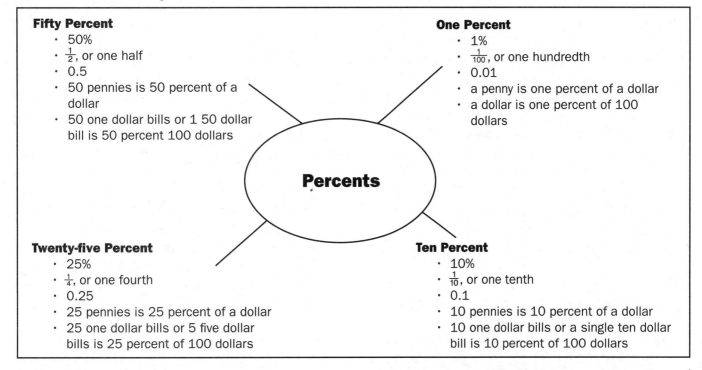

**Fifty Percent**
- 50%
- $\frac{1}{2}$, or one half
- 0.5
- 50 pennies is 50 percent of a dollar
- 50 one dollar bills or 1 50 dollar bill is 50 percent 100 dollars

**One Percent**
- 1%
- $\frac{1}{100}$, or one hundredth
- 0.01
- a penny is one percent of a dollar
- a dollar is one percent of 100 dollars

**Percents**

**Twenty-five Percent**
- 25%
- $\frac{1}{4}$, or one fourth
- 0.25
- 25 pennies is 25 percent of a dollar
- 25 one dollar bills or 5 five dollar bills is 25 percent of 100 dollars

**Ten Percent**
- 10%
- $\frac{1}{10}$, or one tenth
- 0.1
- 10 pennies is 10 percent of a dollar
- 10 one dollar bills or a single ten dollar bill is 10 percent of 100 dollars

# Vocabulary Strategies to Activate Knowledge in Mathematics *(cont.)*

## Semantic Word Map *(cont.)*

### Grades 6–8 Example

**AS = Addition and Subtraction**
- After simplifying inside parentheses, eliminating exponents, and multiplying & dividing, add and subtract as needed.
- $4y + 8 = \dfrac{(6 + 10)^2}{2}$

  $4y + 8 = \dfrac{(16)^2}{2}$

  $4y + 8 = \dfrac{256}{2}$

  $(4y + 8)2 = \dfrac{256(2)}{2}$

$8y + 16 = 256$

$\dfrac{8y + 16}{8} = \dfrac{256}{8}$

$y + 2 = 32$

$y + 2 - 2 = 32 - 2$

$y = 30$

**P = Parenthesis**
- Always begin by simplifying what is inside parentheses before any other operation.
- $y = 6(3 + 7)$

  $y = 6(10)$

  $y = 60$

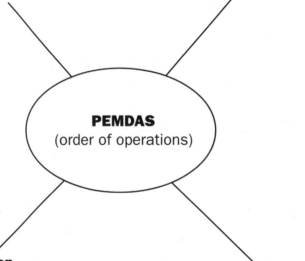

**PEMDAS**
(order of operations)

**MD = Multiplication and Division**
- After simplifying inside parentheses, and eliminating exponents, multiply and divide as needed.
- $4y = \dfrac{(6 + 10)^2}{2}$

  $4y = \dfrac{(16)^2}{2}$

  $4y = \dfrac{256}{2}$

  $4y(2) = \dfrac{256(2)}{2}$

$8y = 256$

$\dfrac{8y}{8} = \dfrac{256}{8}$

$y = 32$

**E = Exponents**
- After simplifying inside parentheses, eliminate exponents
- $y = (6 + 10)^2$

  $y = (16)^2$

  $y = 256$

**Name:** _____

# Semantic Word Map

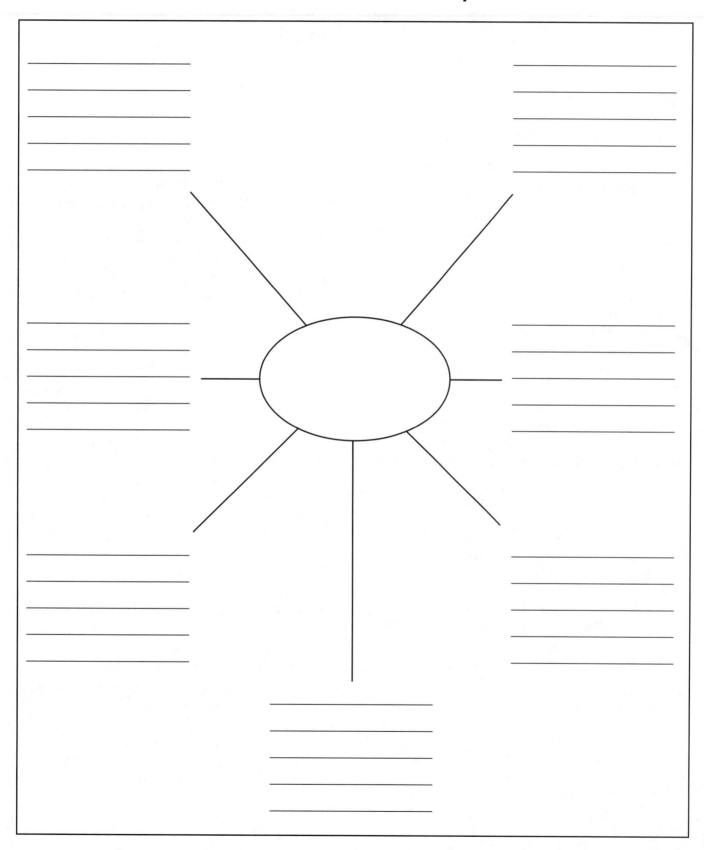

# Vocabulary Strategies to Activate Knowledge in Mathematics *(cont.)*

## Vocabulary Diagram

### Background Information

The Vocabulary Diagram enables students to break down individual words and examine them in different categories. Students look at a given word in terms of its part of speech, its Greek or Latin roots, its synonyms and antonyms, its cognates (related words), the people or things that illustrate the word, a drawing or example, a sentence from their reading, and original sentences. By examining words in this dynamic manner, students gain a clearer understanding of the multidimensional nature of the words they study (Nagy and Scott 2000). Analyzing a single word through different vocabulary categories makes it possible for students to recognize and decode a greater number of unknown words during reading and promotes better long-term retention of vocabulary words. The mathematics teacher should select the target word for this graphic organizer carefully, making sure that the students will be able to complete each category. Students should only complete one Vocabulary Diagram per lesson or perhaps unit, otherwise the word study becomes overwhelming and tedious.

### Grade Levels/Standards Addressed

Grades 3–5 (Standards 5.4, 5.6)
Grades 6–8 (Standards 5.2, 5.3)

### Activity

As students are reading a selection from a mathematics textbook, trade book, or article, locate a dynamic word that is essential to understanding the text. Display a blank overhead transparency of the Vocabulary Diagram (page 63) as a reference guide.

Instruct students to place the selected word in the diamond at the center of their graphic organizers and identify its part of speech. In the rectangle at the bottom left, have students write the sentence from the text that contains the word. Have them locate any synonyms and antonyms for the word and place those in the oval on the left. Next, have students break down the word to identify the Greek or Latin roots and a prefix and suffix, if present. Place these in the oval to the right. Instruct students to find words that have the same Greek or Latin root as the selected word and place them in the trapezoid. Ask them to draw a picture or give an example of the word and put it in the square. Instruct them to think of a person or thing that exemplifies the word and add this to the circle. In the rectangle at the bottom right, ask students to write one or two original sentences that clearly demonstrate the word's definition. As a class, share ideas on the blank overhead, and discuss each word as needed.

### Differentiation

Complete some portions of the Vocabulary Diagram sheet for ELLs and below-level students to allow them to concentrate on other areas (i.e., synonyms, antonyms, parts of speech, and roots). They will also benefit from whole classroom instruction and completion of the diagram. Gifted students should be encouraged to independently select a word that they find challenging and complete the form independently.

# Vocabulary Strategies to Activate Knowledge in Mathematics *(cont.)*

## Vocabulary Diagram *(cont.)*

**Grades 3–5 Example**

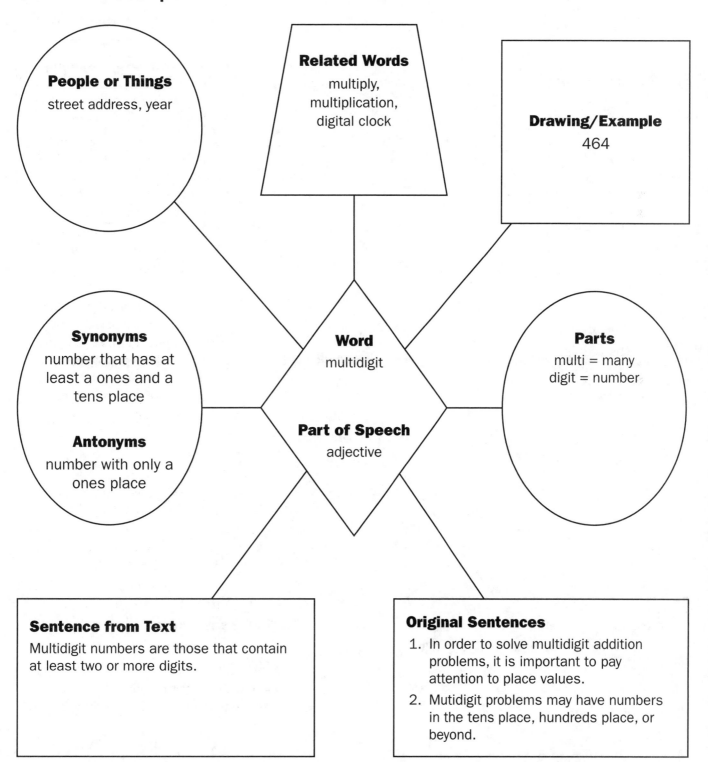

**People or Things**
street address, year

**Related Words**
multiply,
multiplication,
digital clock

**Drawing/Example**
464

**Synonyms**
number that has at
least a ones and a
tens place

**Antonyms**
number with only a
ones place

**Word**
multidigit

**Part of Speech**
adjective

**Parts**
multi = many
digit = number

**Sentence from Text**
Multidigit numbers are those that contain
at least two or more digits.

**Original Sentences**
1. In order to solve multidigit addition
   problems, it is important to pay
   attention to place values.
2. Mutidigit problems may have numbers
   in the tens place, hundreds place, or
   beyond.

# Vocabulary Strategies to Activate Knowledge
## in Mathematics *(cont.)*

## Vocabulary Diagram *(cont.)*

**Grades 6–8 Example**

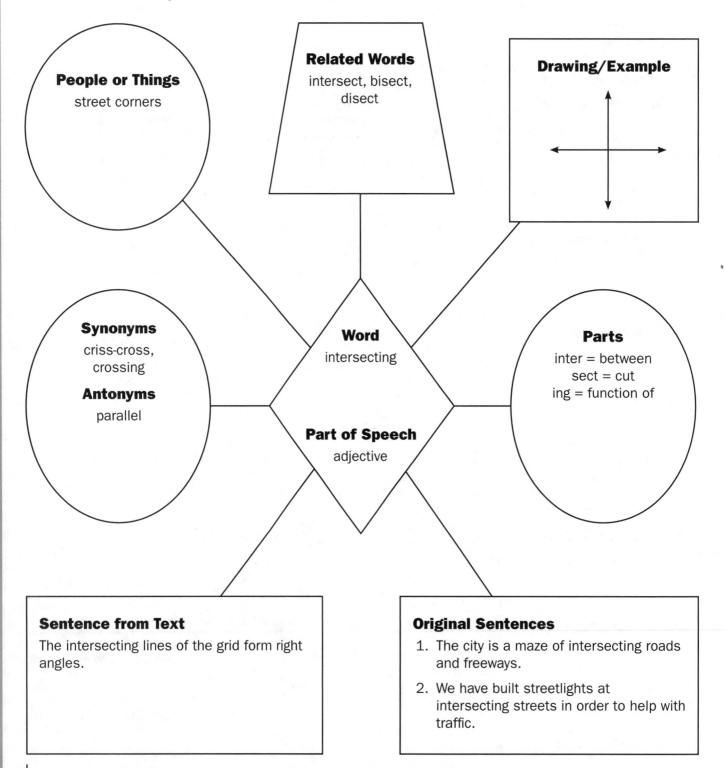

**People or Things**
street corners

**Related Words**
intersect, bisect, disect

**Drawing/Example**

**Synonyms**
criss-cross, crossing

**Antonyms**
parallel

**Word**
intersecting

**Part of Speech**
adjective

**Parts**
inter = between
sect = cut
ing = function of

**Sentence from Text**
The intersecting lines of the grid form right angles.

**Original Sentences**
1. The city is a maze of intersecting roads and freeways.
2. We have built streetlights at intersecting streets in order to help with traffic.

**Name:** _____

# Vocabulary Diagram

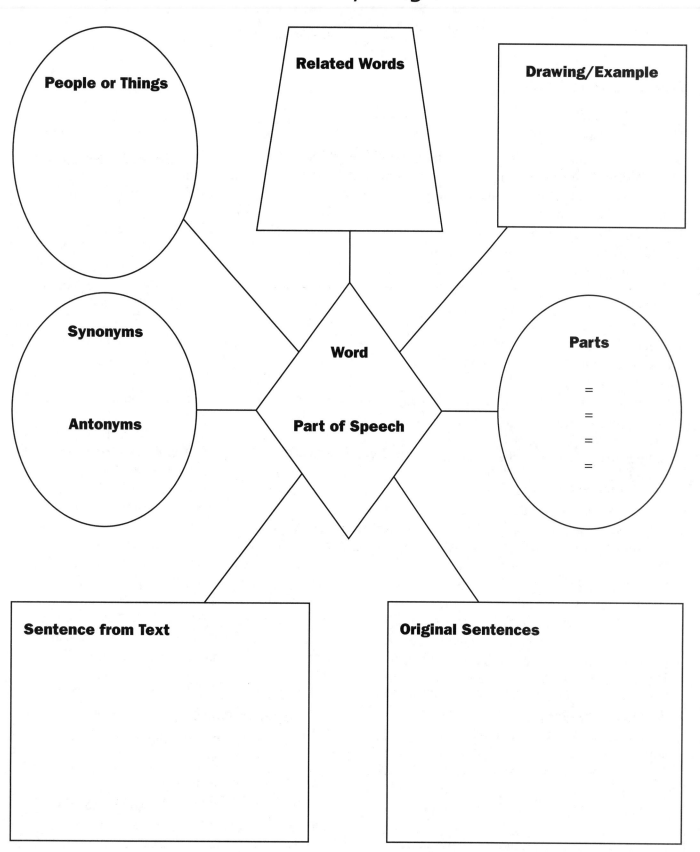

**People or Things**

**Related Words**

**Drawing/Example**

**Synonyms**

**Antonyms**

**Word**

**Part of Speech**

**Parts**

=

=

=

=

**Sentence from Text**

**Original Sentences**

# Using and Building Prior Knowledge in Mathematics

## What Is Prior Knowledge?

Students learn more effectively when they already know a little something about a topic and when the concepts involved in the topic mean something to them. Research on enriching background knowledge has demonstrated that activating such knowledge increases comprehension (Christen and Murphy 1991). Linking new information to the students' prior knowledge activates students' interest and curiosity and gives instruction a sense of purpose. Furthermore, building upon students' familiarity with a topic enables the students to connect the curriculum content to their personal lives and experiences. Using and building prior knowledge during mathematics reading tasks is essential to improving reading comprehension skills. There are a number of strategies mathematics teachers can utilize to make this happen.

But what is prior knowledge? Experts often use the words *schema, schemata,* and *schema theory* when discussing prior knowledge, but many teachers do not know exactly what these terms mean. It is important to understand that when one reads, one associates any new information with information that one already knows. Researchers have established that readers build a *schema*, or a mental representation, of what they learn to organize their prior knowledge on a topic. A schema is essentially a large database in the brain that holds all of an individual's experiences and knowledge. This means the new information that one acquires from reading must be associated with and connected to the prior knowledge that one already has. This is known as the spiral of knowledge (Poplin 1988, as cited by Dechant 1991). Because of this, the newly constructed meaning that the reader forms is a product of the transformation that occurs between the new experience being learned and all other previous experiences (Dechant 1991). *Schema theory* provides an explanation for how information is stored in the mind. *Schemata* is the plural for schema, so imagine that individuals hold a number of databases in their brains. When one learns something new, one finds a database and looks through the database to find the right column and row to store the new information. Once the new information is placed in the desired location, one sees the information in the column and row in a whole new way. One may even look at the entire database in a whole new way.

Dechant (1991) explains that researchers generally use the term *assimilation* to describe the ways individuals fit new information in with old information. Every new experience one has is related to and becomes a part of one's previous experience, which in turn becomes the basis for new understandings and meanings. When readers come across new information, they may incorporate it into their existing schema by merely attaching it to the existing organizational structures. Researchers since Piaget have called this assimilation, but recent scholarship refers to it as *accretion*. Sometimes, it is necessary to alter the schema slightly to accommodate the new information. This is known as *accommodation*, but recent cognitive psychologists refer to this as *tuning*. At other times, it is necessary to restructure the schemata entirely when readers cannot make sense of what they are reading with their existing schemata. *Restructuring* is the term most commonly used for this process.

# Using and Building Prior Knowledge in Mathematics *(cont.)*

## What Is Prior Knowledge? *(cont.)*

Reading comprehension is not just affected by prior knowledge or experience with the topic being learned. Prior knowledge is a combination of students' established attitudes, experience, and knowledge (Kujawa and Huske 1995) as explained below:

### Attitudes

- beliefs about themselves as learners/readers
- awareness of their individual interests and strengths
- motivation and their desire to read

### Experiences

- everyday activities that relate to reading
- events in their lives that provide background understanding
- family and community experiences that they bring to school with them

### Knowledge

- of the reading process itself
- of content (geometry and data analysis)
- of topics (regrouping and fractions)
- of concepts (estimation and numeration)
- of different types of style and form (fiction and nonfiction)
- of text structure (textbook page or glossary)
- of the academic and personal goals

It is generally accepted that the more elaborate the schemata, the richer the learning experience for the students. The breadth and depth of the prior knowledge that students bring to the classroom is strongly connected to their achievement in reading. But what happens when students do not have adequate prior knowledge on the topics that mathematics teachers present? It is the teacher's responsibility to activate and build on the prior knowledge of the students in order to help them comprehend the new information. Teachers must set up the schemata so students can place the new information in the columns and rows of their databases as needed.

Generally, teachers begin each term or year by formally and informally assessing the students' attitudes toward learning, reading, and themselves, as well as their experiences and knowledge about a wide variety of topics. Having this basic information about each child helps teachers differentiate instruction and helps increase motivation. The more teachers know about their students, the better they can prepare to teach them.

# Using and Building Prior Knowledge in Mathematics *(cont.)*

## Assimilation of Knowledge

To make this clear, consider this example from mathematics learning. When students first learn about numbers, they may merely learn how to count from 1 to 10. This event establishes their schema about numbers. Later, students may learn what the different numbers look like, meaning the shape and configuration of them, and they will assimilate the information into their existing schema about the sequence that they previously learned. This establishes a connection in their brain. As students learn more about numbers, they will likely learn one-to-one correspondence, meaning they will learn what the number 1 means in terms of 1 teddy bear versus 2 teddy bears versus 3 teddy bears and so on. At this time, students may have difficulty distinguishing numbers from letters, and if asked after a demonstration (in which letters are paired with numbers), students may confuse the sounds of the letters with the physical representations of numbers. Therefore, students must alter their schema about numbers to accommodate the different information. At some point, students will learn the many ways in which numbers relate to one another through addition and subtraction. Later, students will learn multiplication and division. Later still, students will learn fractions, percentages, ratios, and eventually, algebra. This later stage may require them to restructure their schema altogether because they may not understand how to introduce the concept of letters as variables into their schema of numbers and mathematics.

## What Good Teachers Do

Researchers have developed guidelines for teachers to help students actively link new knowledge to existing knowledge (Readence, Bean, and Baldwin 2000). Following these guidelines also increases student motivation.

To help students actively link new knowledge to existing knowledge:

- Provide a supportive, well-structured classroom environment.

- Give assignments that are meaningful and challenging but not frustrating.

- Break up complex, lengthy tasks into manageable increments.

- Teach students to set realistic goals.

- Provide explicit, immediate feedback.

- Reward success through pleasurable activities, points, or praise.

- Provide opportunities for active student responses to text.

# Using and Building Prior Knowledge in Mathematics *(cont.)*

## Shared Learning Experiences

The best way to build on prior knowledge is to create shared learning experiences for the students. Let's say the new mathematics unit for first graders is about geometric shapes. The teacher can hold a class discussion in which the students answer questions. The teacher might record shared ideas on the board as a brainstorm to activate students' knowledge about geometric shapes. Some of the students may have little prior knowledge about geometric shapes, while other students may have attended preschool or Kindergarten and have a solid foundation of knowledge about them. Regardless of the prior knowledge of the students, creating shared learning experiences in which background information is activated provides all students with enough information to effectively read and learn about new concepts. The following are some ways to create shared learning experiences:

- demonstrations (tracing shapes onto large sheets of paper and cutting them out in front of students)

- role-playing or theatrical performances (forming shapes with their bodies)

- hands-on activities (gluing macaroni onto paper that has the shape outlined on it)

- independent research (bringing things from home that represent various shapes)

- debates (discussing the similarities of a pyramid with both a triangle and a square)

- visuals (pictures, posters, etc.)

- read alouds (shape picture books)

- freewriting (writing about three-dimensional shapes in everyday items)

In a unit about shapes, any or all of these ideas can be combined to help create a volume of shared experiences about the topic. The same can also be done with varying math concepts across all grade levels. To teach the concept of fractions to second graders, provide a cake or a pizza as a demonstration. For third graders, have them create a theatrical production that teaches figuring out unit cost when given total cost. For example, one of the children must make 20 pizzas for the entire grade. He goes to the baker and is able to buy 20 pizza crusts for $35.00. The class must figure out the cost of each crust. The skit could continue until the individual costs of all the ingredients were determined. With fourth graders, take them to the play area and have them do a hands-on activity where they calculate the area of a given portion of the blacktop or grass. With fifth graders, have them do some independent research at home or in class on the computer to find data on precipitation levels or population, and then use the information to compare data using fractions or percentages. With sixth graders, provide a complicated word problem and then have them debate as to which math strategy they feel would best solve the problem. With seventh graders, provide a visual for the order of operations (like a poster) and discuss it with the class. Have eighth graders research biographies of famous mathematicians and read the portion to the class that they found most interesting. Use any or all of these topics for freewriting. This sharing of experiences and ideas leads to greater development of background knowledge, which in turn leads to greater comprehension.

> The best way to build on prior knowledge is through shared learning experiences.

# Strategies to Assess and Build on Prior Knowledge in Mathematics

## KWL Chart

### Background Information

The KWL Chart is a three-part strategy to encourage active reading that was first described by Donna Ogle in 1986. The strategy involves recording ideas during each of the three stages of the reading process: pre-reading, during reading, and post-reading. During the pre-reading stage, students are asked to explain what they know about the topic they will be reading about. This part of the chart (K) stands for "What I Know." This stage is used to activate prior knowledge. As students share their ideas, it is typical for some disagreements to occur, and they begin to question what they know. From these disagreements, teachers can help the students formulate questions to clarify any uncertainty they may have. In the during-reading stage, students again are asked what they wonder or want to find out in further reading. This part of the chart (W) stands for "What I Want to Know." During the post-reading stage, students explain what they have learned from the reading and other activities, and the class discusses what has been learned, which questions have been answered, and what new questions have emerged. This part of the chart (L) stands for "What I Learned." The KWL activity makes it possible for teachers to model an interactive study approach for students.

Students in the primary grades can complete a KWL Chart as a class. Older students can complete KWLs independently, but at the end of completing each column, the teacher should gather together the students' ideas, questions, and answers so that all students can review the information together. Questions can be recorded using a variety of methods. Teachers can use a transparency of a KWL Chart and record student responses for the class to review, but this is a temporary recording. Teachers can record questions on chart paper, which can be displayed in the classroom to make a permanent record of the students' questions.

For young learners, teachers also can record the questions on sentence strips and insert each question into a pocket chart. An advantage in using a pocket chart is that questions can be added, rearranged, grouped, and used for other purposes during subsequent stages of an investigation. Using graphic organizer software and a projector can be a highly effective strategy for gathering, sorting, and sharing information during the span of an investigation for students at all levels.

### Grade Levels/Standards Addressed

Grades 1–2 (Standards 7.1, 7.4)
Grades 3–5 (Standards 7.1, 7.6)
Grades 6–8 (Standards 7.1, 7.4)

### Activity

Recreate the KWL Chart (page 71) on a large piece of chart paper and display it for the class to view. Before beginning a unit in mathematics, ask students to brainstorm everything they know about the topic of study. While recording their ideas in the K column, ask students probing questions to activate any prior knowledge they may have about the topic of study. Encourage students to make connections between the information and their prior experiences. Students may present conflicting information and may begin to question what they know, but do not correct any false information provided by the students at this stage. Help students develop questions to clear up any uncertainty that they may have. Write these questions in the W column.

# Strategies to Assess and Build on Prior Knowledge in Mathematics (cont.)

## KWL Chart (cont.)

### Activity (cont.)

Next, present students with a reading selection on the topic of study. As students read, encourage them to articulate anything they may wonder about or want to find out more about through additional research and reading. Record their ideas in the W column below the questions they have already generated. After students complete the reading, present the partially completed KWL Chart again, but this time ask them to review the information in the K and W columns. Have students discuss what they learned from the reading, answer the questions they generated prior to reading, and generate additional questions that they feel should be addressed in further study. Record items of note from the discussion in the L column. Be sure to post the KWL Chart in the classroom throughout the unit to guide students in their studies.

### Variations

The KWL Chart can be extended to include other categories or columns:

#### Categories of Information

Mathematics teachers can add another area to the chart to include Categories of Information We Expect to See. With this addition, teachers can use the KWL Chart to help students anticipate the categories of information the author may provide in the reading selection. The teacher and students should use the information recorded in the K column to help see the potential categories within their prior knowledge.

#### H—How to Find Out

Another extension involves adding an H for a How to Find Out column to create a KWHL Chart. Asking students to articulate how they will search for answers to their mathematics questions encourages them to develop strong research skills.

#### S—Still Want to Learn

Another extension involves adding an S category to enable students to explore what they still want to learn. Adding the Still Want to Learn category encourages students to explore mathematics topics independently and in more depth.

### Differentiation

Give ELLs time to discuss their prior knowledge and what they wonder about with a partner or in a small group before they share in a large group discussion. This will allow them more time to practice and will reduce any anxiety they may feel. Gifted students may inadvertently dominate the class discussion when adding to the K column if they have a great deal of prior knowledge, so ask them to write an essay or generate their own list of knowledge independent of the class. Invite these students to independently explore the topics of further study generated by the class during the W stage and report their findings later. Prior to introducing a new unit of study, inform students reading below grade level of the next topic of study. Provide them with additional time to build any prior knowledge on the topic, which may assist them in the reading task.

# Strategies to Assess and Build on Prior Knowledge in Mathematics *(cont.)*

## KWL Chart *(cont.)*

### Grades 1–2 Example
**Topic: <u>Inequalities</u>**

| K | W | L |
|---|---|---|
| 10 is greater than 1 | What is the symbol for greater than? | > |
| 22 is less than 24 | What is the symbol for less than? | < |
| 64 is less than 100 | How can you tell which symbol to use? | If you think of the opening as a mouth, the mouth always wants to eat the bigger number. |

### Grades 3–5 Example
**Topic: <u>Place Value</u>**

| K | W | L |
|---|---|---|
| in the number 5,984,762; the 2 is the ones place<br>the 6 is in the tens place<br>the 7 is in the hundreds place<br>the 4 is in the thousands place | What is the name of the place value for the 8? | ten thousands place |
| | What is the name of the place value for the 9? | hundred thousands place |
| | What is the name of the place value for the 5? | millions place |

### Grades 6–8 Example
**Topic: <u>Multiplying Binomials</u>**

| K | W | L |
|---|---|---|
| the distributive property | What does FOIL mean? | First, Outer, Inner, & Last |
| $4(x + y)$ would be $4x + 4y$ | When is FOIL used? | used for multiplying two binomials |
| $4x + 4y$ is a binomial | | i.e., $(4x + 4y)(3x - 2y)$<br>Multiply the first 2 terms: $4x \cdot 3x = 12x^2$<br>Multiply the outer 2 terms: $4x \cdot -2y = -8xy$<br>Multiply the inner 2 terms: $4y \cdot 3x = 12xy$<br>Multiply the last 2 terms: $4y \cdot -2y = -8y^2$<br>Combine like terms and answer is<br>$12x^2 + 4xy - 8y^2$ |

**Name:** _____

**Topic:** _____

# KWL Chart

| K | W | L |
|---|---|---|
|   |   |   |

# Strategies to Assess and Build on Prior Knowledge in Mathematics *(cont.)*

## Concept Map

### Background Information

A Concept Map is a graphic representation of the information related to a concept or concepts discussed in mathematics texts (West, Farmer, and Wolff 1991). Teachers often construct a Concept Map about the new reading material and present it to the class prior to reading. In doing so, teachers better prepare the students to understand what they are reading. As students read from their text, they can incorporate the relationships or links among the new concepts learned in the Concept Map.

There are many variations to the Concept Map, and some may suggest that it is merely a visual representation of traditional outlining, but Concept Maps allow students to learn more than just facts. The Concept Map allows students to develop organizational skills because they can view the concepts and details in terms of how they are related to one another in a visual, hierarchical format. Using a Concept Map helps students develop strong organizational skills in their writing as well. Generally, the information presented in a Concept Map is hierarchical, so it moves from general categories to specific details. The appearance is similar to a flow chart in that the links between the concepts are demonstrated through lines and arrows. This structure can help students plan out the organization of paragraphs rather easily. Please note that students should use the same shapes (circles, rectangles, ovals, etc.) in their Concept Maps to represent the same categories of information.

There are several variations to the Concept Map (page 74): Spider Maps (page 75), Chain Maps, Hierarchy Maps, etc., but all are essentially the same.

### Grade Levels/Standards Addressed

Grades 3–5 (Standards 7.1, 7.6)
Grades 6–8 (Standards 7.1, 7.4)

### Preparation

Begin the process by conducting a thorough reading of the material that students will be expected to read. Identify the most important concepts that are directly related to the teaching objectives in the reading, and note the concepts, words, and phrases that are related to these important concepts. Then organize the concepts and identify the relationships and connections among those concepts. Next choose a descriptive title that generates interest and increases curiosity. Organize the concepts and details into different categories. It may help to place the title and the terms on separate slips of paper so that they can be manipulated in various ways to demonstrate the links and relationships. The last stage in the process is to refine the information presented in the map to enhance the students' learning. It is important to keep the amount of information presented simple to minimize confusion. Use the different shapes for different categories of information to demonstrate the hierarchical relationships among the concepts, information, and details. Make sure to leave adequate room for students to add their prior knowledge to the map.

# Strategies to Assess and Build on Prior Knowledge in Mathematics *(cont.)*

## Concept Map *(cont.)*

### Activity

Begin by presenting the Concept Map to the class to prepare students for a selected reading. It is best to provide students with a blank map so that they can write down the information presented. Plan to use an overhead version of the map and either fill it out using notes as you present the information or display the concepts one at a time by covering up the transparency with a sheet (or sheets) of paper that you can move around as you discuss each concept. This will reduce the amount of information presented to the students at any given time and will enable them to focus more intently on the concepts you discuss.

Start with a clear explanation of the purpose of a Concept Map and explain how the map can be effectively used as a learning tool. Read the title and ask the students to predict what concepts may be presented in relation to the main topic of inquiry.

As you present the information on the map, encourage students to become more actively involved by asking them to share their prior knowledge and ideas related to the information. Incorporate their information on the map. Use the presentation time to clarify any misinformation and determine the level of prior knowledge the students have developed on the topic.

While students read the selection, they can use the Concept Map as a study guide. They can add information to their maps by taking notes or highlighting pertinent information.

### Variation

List all of the terms and categories that belong in a concept map prior to presenting it to the students. Distribute blank pieces of paper to the students, and ask them to create a concept map using the list.

### Differentiation

When students complete Concept Maps independently, it is important to scaffold the map for ELLs and students reading below grade level. Provide some of the concepts for them in the blank map to help guide them as they fill out the map independently. It may also help both groups to place the students in pairs so that they can work cooperatively to complete the map. It is important in both cases that the teacher review the maps completed independently as a class to discuss the variations in the connections and organizational structure that students create. Gifted students may need very little instruction to complete Concept Maps independently. They should be encouraged to add another dimension to their organization—color.

# Strategies to Assess and Build on
# Prior Knowledge in Mathematics *(cont.)*

## Concept Map *(cont.)*

**Grades 3–5 Example (after presentation)**

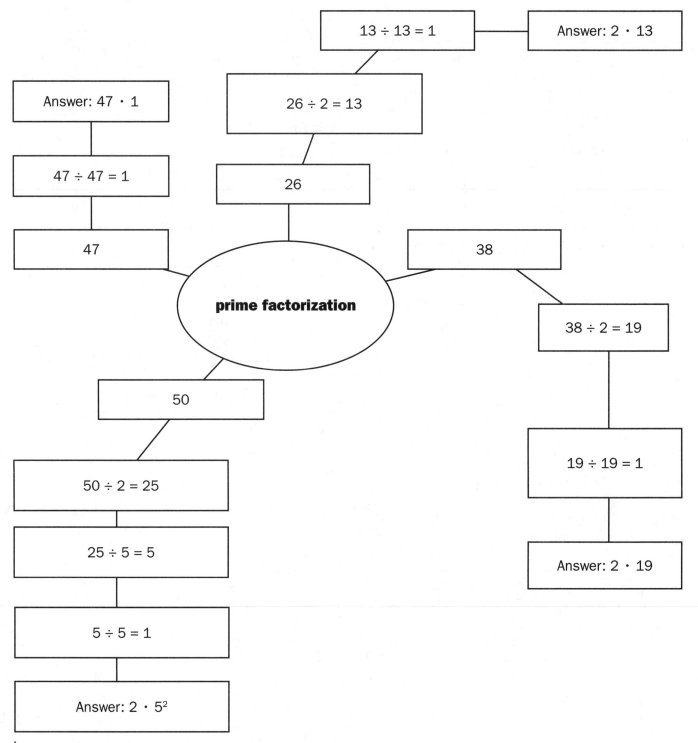

# Strategies to Assess and Build on Prior Knowledge in Mathematics *(cont.)*

## Concept Map *(cont.)*

**Grades 6–8 Example  (homework assignment)**

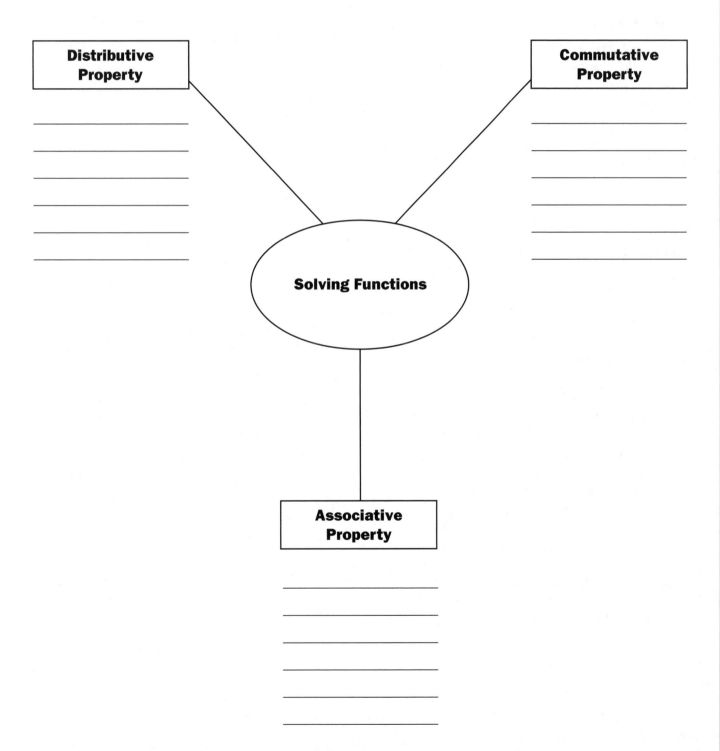

# Strategies to Assess and Build on Prior Knowledge in Mathematics (cont.)

## Frame

### Background Information

A Frame is a chart that is designed to organize important information in rows and columns. It can appear as a matrix, grid, or framework of some sort that shows the relationship between the main ideas, concepts, and details. This strategy is very helpful when students are learning how to distinguish essential concepts and details from each other because it allows students to quickly compare and contrast information.

There are different types of Frames that work best in different reading situations (Ryder and Graves 2003). Matrix Frames are best used in mathematics classes for comparing and contrasting information, examining cause-and-effect relationships, and analyzing forms and their functions.

Once the column and row topics are identified, Frames can be effective tools to activate prior knowledge in students prior to reading. Teachers can also fill out all columns and rows and present the information as a preview for reading, which better prepares students to comprehend new information. Teachers may choose to present a blank Frame to students with the column and row topics selected, then provide the information to be placed within each Frame in a list. Students can then determine which items appear in each Frame.

Frames also can serve as an effective activity to help students improve their writing skills in mathematics. The nature of Frames naturally help students organize and structure information.

When students write summaries based on the information in the Frame, it allows them to reflect on the content, elaborate on the application, and note relationships or draw distinctions between concepts and information (Ryder and Graves 2003).

### Grade Levels/Standards Addressed

Grades 3–5 (Standards 7.1, 7.6)
Grades 6–8 (Standards 7.1, 7.4)

### Preparation

Review the mathematics materials with extra care and identify the major ideas and concepts in the reading. Next, consider how the concepts or main ideas can be compared, what features they share, and what specific features or characteristics they possess (Ryder and Graves 2003). Draw the Frame by creating and labeling the rows and columns. The main topics, ideas, and concepts usually appear in the rows, while the categories for the characteristics and/or relationships appear in the columns. Fill in each of the empty slots with the information for use in class.

# Strategies to Assess and Build on
# Prior Knowledge in Mathematics *(cont.)*

## Frame *(cont.)*

### Activity

After carefully reviewing the student reading materials, determine the topics for the columns and rows, and complete each slot of the Frame. Distribute blank copies of the Frame (page 79) and draw on students' previous experiences to help build their prior knowledge on the topic. After reviewing the Frame, have students complete the reading. They can use the Frame to help them review what they have read.

### Variation

Prepare a Frame on an overhead transparency to present to the students prior to reading about a new concept. Select the topics for each column and row, but do not fill in each slot with the necessary information. Instead, place the information that belongs in each column in a list of items, and ask the students to use their prior knowledge to place the items in the list in the correct slots. After the students complete the reading, review the Frame and correct any errors.

### Differentiation

ELLs will need visual input to support their understanding of the new information while the matrix frame is presented. Students reading below grade level should not receive a blank matrix frame to complete, but should be given one that is partially complete to help orient them to the task and to prevent them from feeling overwhelmed by the task. Gifted students may wish to complete the matrix frame independently while they are reading.

# Strategies to Assess and Build on Prior Knowledge in Mathematics (cont.)

## Frame (cont.)

**Grades 3–5 Example**

### Topic: Expanded Notation

| Numbers | Hundred Thousands | + Ten Thousands | + Thousands | + Hundreds | + Tens | + Ones |
|---------|-------------------|-----------------|-------------|------------|--------|--------|
| 542,125 | 500,000 | + 40,000 | + 2,000 | + 100 | + 20 | + 5 |
| 874,451 | 800,000 | + 70,000 | + 4,000 | + 400 | + 50 | + 1 |
| 802,354 | 800,000 | | + 2,000 | + 300 | + 50 | + 4 |
| 20,154 | | 20,000 | | + 100 | + 50 | + 4 |

**Grades 6–8 Example**

### Topic: Linear Functions

| Equations | y = mx + b | slope (m) | direction | x-intercept | y-intercept |
|-----------|------------|-----------|-----------|-------------|-------------|
| $y = 14 + 7x$ | $y = 7x + 14$ | $m = 7$ | up | $-2$ | 14 |
| $3y = 24 - 6x$ | $y = -2x + 8$ | $m = -2$ | down | 4 | 8 |
| $6y - 3x = 2$ | $y = \frac{1}{2}x + \frac{1}{3}$ | $m = \frac{1}{2}$ | up | $-\frac{2}{3}$ | $\frac{1}{3}$ |

**Name:** _____

# Frame

**Directions:** Write in the topic for the Frame and the titles for each column. Then fill in each box with information from the text.

**Topic:** _____

| | | | |
|---|---|---|---|
| | | | |
| | | | |
| | | | |
| | | | |
| | | | |
| | | | |

# Strategies to Assess and Build on Prior Knowledge in Mathematics *(cont.)*

## List-Group-Label

### Background Information

List-Group-Label is an activity that can be used in mathematics to assess and build on prior knowledge. It combines brainstorming and classification as a way to help students organize concepts related to mathematics reading. Students associate their knowledge with concepts presented by the teacher, and then they organize the information by generating categories. It works best when students have some background knowledge related to the concepts, but it can also be used to introduce or review concepts.

The activity stimulates meaningful associations among vocabulary and concepts that are a part of the same category. It also helps students to coordinate the hierarchical relationships among concept words. This activity gives students the opportunity to apply different processes to the same values as well. Most importantly, it activates students' mathematics background knowledge prior to reading the new text.

Most importantly, the students must justify the categories they have selected by presenting a rationale. The teacher must keep the students focused on words and categories that are directly related to the lesson objectives. The more the students describe and explain their rationales for the categories and words selected, the more the students will make associations with new words.

### Grade Levels/Standards Addressed

Grades 1–2 (Standards 7.3, 7.4)
Grades 3–5 (Standards 7.1, 7.6)
Grades 6–8 (Standards 7.1, 7.4)

### Activity

Write the word or phrase that describes the lesson topic on the board or a transparency. Ask students to generate words, phrases, or numbers associated with the topic, and write their responses in a list. If students give an item that is seemingly unrelated to the topic, ask them to explain the connection and encourage them to make stronger connections. Once students have generated 20–30 items, divide the class into small groups and distribute List-Group-Label graphic organizers (page 83). Have students organize those words that will fit into categories and eliminate words that do not belong. The category labels should be determined by evaluating the different attributes, characteristics, and features that the words may have in common. Students may generate additional words for the categories and reorganize the categories and words by combining categories or deleting categories.

### Variations

Present the class with a list of words, phrases, or numbers, and ask students individually or in small groups to classify the words and select the labels for those categories.

### Differentiation

ELLs may benefit from having resource books available to them during the word-generating process so that they can locate words. Use several words to explain each word associated with the topic—providing visuals if possible—so that ELLs can better understand. Clearly define the words on the board for students reading below grade level. Both ELLs and students reading below grade level will benefit from working in mixed-ability groups. Encourage gifted students to reclassify the words into alternate categories.

# Strategies to Assess and Build on Prior Knowledge in Mathematics (cont.)

## List-Group-Label (cont.)

### Grades 1–2 Example

**Topic: Time**

**List**

| | | | | | | |
|---|---|---|---|---|---|---|
| 5:00 P.M. | 8:30 A.M. | 12:00 P.M. | 6:30 P.M. | 3:30 A.M. | 9:00 A.M. | 8:00 P.M. |
| 1:30 A.M. | 6:00 P.M. | 2:30 P.M. | 4:30 A.M. | 7:00 A.M. | 11:00 P.M. | 10:30 A.M. |
| 1:00 P.M. | 4:30 P.M. | 2:30 A.M. | 3:00 A.M. | 9:30 A.M. | 1:30 P.M. | 7:30 A.M. |

**Categories**

| Morning | Afternoon | Night/Evening |
|---|---|---|
| 8:30 A.M. | 12:00 P.M. | 5:00 P.M. |
| 9:00 A.M. | 2:30 P.M. | 6:30 P.M. |
| 7:00 A.M. | 1:00 P.M. | 3:30 A.M. |
| 10:30 A.M. | 4:30 P.M. | 8:00 P.M. |
| 9:30 A.M. | 1:30 P.M. | 1:30 A.M. |
| 7:30 A.M. | | 6:00 P.M. |
| 4:30 A.M. | | 11:00 P.M. |
| | | 2:30 A.M. |
| | | 3:00 A.M. |

### Grades 3–5 Example

**Topic: Rounding**

**List**

| | | | | |
|---|---|---|---|---|
| 45,251 | 65,256 | 5,487 | 654 | 87,654 |

**Categories**

| Original Number | Ten Thousands | Thousands | Hundreds | Tens |
|---|---|---|---|---|
| 45,251 | 50,000 | 45,000 | 45,300 | 45,250 |
| 65,256 | 70,000 | 65,000 | 65,300 | 65,260 |
| 5,487 | N/A | 5,000 | 5,500 | 5,490 |
| 654 | N/A | N/A | 700 | 650 |
| 87,654 | 90,000 | 88,000 | 87,700 | 87,750 |

# Strategies to Assess and Build on Prior Knowledge in Mathematics (cont.)

## List-Group-Label (cont.)

### Grades 6–8 Example

**Topic: <u>Sporting Goods Sale</u>**

**List**

| | | | |
|---|---|---|---|
| jacket - $25.50 | boots - $124.99 | snow hat - $12.99 | surfboard - $325.00 |
| wet suit - $59.99 | pack of socks - $2.99 | hiking shoes - $84.99 | skis - $329.99 |
| gloves - $19.99 | pants - $49.99 | shirt - $35.50 | towel - $15.99 |
| goggles - $18.99 | soccer ball - $22.00 | sun umbrella - $159.99 | basketball - $22.99 |
| jersey - $34.99 | shin guards - $42.99 | helmet - $87.00 | beach chair - $19.50 |

**Categories**

| Original Item & Cost | 10% off | 20% off | 30% off | 50% off |
|---|---|---|---|---|
| jacket - $25.50 | $22.95 | $20.40 | $17.85 | $12.75 |
| boots - $124.99 | $112.49 | $99.99 | $87.49 | $62.50 |
| snow hat - $12.99 | $11.69 | $10.39 | $9.09 | $6.50 |
| surfboard - $325.00 | $292.50 | $260.00 | $227.50 | $162.50 |
| wet suit - $59.99 | $53.99 | $47.99 | $41.99 | $30.00 |
| pack of socks - $2.99 | $2.69 | $2.39 | $2.09 | $1.50 |
| hiking shoes - $84.99 | $76.49 | $67.99 | $59.49 | $42.50 |
| skis - $329.99 | $296.99 | $263.99 | $230.99 | $165.00 |
| gloves - $19.99 | $17.99 | $15.99 | $13.99 | $10.00 |
| pants - $49.99 | $44.99 | $39.99 | $34.99 | $25.00 |
| shirt - $35.50 | $31.95 | $28.40 | $24.85 | $17.75 |
| towel - $15.99 | $14.39 | $12.79 | $11.19 | $8.00 |
| goggles - $18.99 | $17.09 | $15.19 | $13.29 | $9.50 |
| soccer ball - $22.00 | $19.80 | $17.60 | $15.40 | $11.00 |
| sun umbrella - $159.99 | $143.99 | $127.99 | $111.99 | $80.00 |
| basketball - $22.99 | $20.69 | $18.39 | $16.09 | $11.50 |
| jersey - $34.99 | $31.49 | $27.99 | $24.49 | $17.50 |
| shin guards - $42.99 | $38.69 | $34.39 | $30.09 | $21.50 |
| helmet - $87.00 | $78.30 | $69.60 | $60.90 | $43.50 |
| beach chair - $19.50 | $17.55 | $15.60 | $13.65 | $9.75 |

**Name:** _____

# List-Group-Label

**Directions:** Write in the topic, then make a list of words about the topic. Look at the list and create categories of related words. Be sure to label each category.

**Topic:** _____

**List**

_____    _____    _____

_____    _____    _____

_____    _____    _____

_____    _____    _____

_____    _____    _____

_____    _____    _____

_____    _____    _____

**Categories**

_____    _____    _____

_____    _____    _____

_____    _____    _____

_____    _____    _____

_____    _____    _____

_____    _____    _____

# Strategies to Assess and Build on
# Prior Knowledge in Mathematics *(cont.)*

# Think Sheet

## Background Information

The Think Sheet strategy enables students to compare and contrast their pre-reading ideas with their post-reading understandings. Teachers encourage students to examine their own background knowledge and questions on mathematics issues to be studied so that they will be better prepared to read. After reading, when students compare and contrast their ideas and questions with the new information in the reading materials, they are better able to make connections between their prior knowledge and their new conceptual knowledge. This technique helps new mathematics information remain in the long-term memory because the students have made the connections among their schemata.

This strategy works best when there is an issue that involves some debate or controversy. The teacher models the process on an overhead transparency so that students better understand the procedure. The teacher should take some time to explain that mathematics reading generally centers on an issue or topic about which the reader may have many questions.

## Activity

Determine the main topic of the selected passage. Distribute copies of the Think Sheet (page 87) to the students or recreate one on an overhead transparency or on the board. Present the main issue to the class, and ask students to generate questions that they have about the topic. Ask them to explain what they hope to learn from reading. Write their questions down in the first column, "My Questions." Next, ask students to explain what they already know about the main issue, and encourage them to share even if they are not sure if their information is correct. Write their information in the second column, "My Thoughts." Explain to the students that they should read the text to locate the answers to their questions and also to determine if their thoughts were supported or countered by the information in the text. As the students read, they record the important ideas from the text in the last column on the Think Sheet ("Text Ideas"). After they have completed the reading, students share what they have learned from the reading and make connections between their questions, their thoughts, and the information presented in the text.

## Grade Levels/Standards Addressed

Grades 1–2 (Standards 7.3, 7.4)
Grades 3–5 (Standards 7.1, 7.6)
Grades 6–8 (Standards 7.1, 7.4)

# Strategies to Assess and Build on Prior Knowledge in Mathematics (cont.)

## Think Sheet (cont.)

### Activity (cont.)

The reading can be completed as a read aloud for younger students (1–2), a paired reading for middle grades (3–5), or as a homework assignment for older students (6–8). Discuss what students learned from the reading, and show them how their questions, their thoughts, and the information in the text are all related and connected. Ask questions such as: *What did the book say about your question? Did you have any questions that were not answered by the book? Were any of your thoughts inaccurate? Which ones?*

### Differentiation

Model how to formulate questions for ELLs. Gifted students should be encouraged to conduct further reading to find the answers to any questions left unanswered by the reading selection and share their findings with the class. Scaffold the Think Sheet with some responses for students reading below grade level, and allow them to do a paired reading or hear the reading selection aloud.

# Strategies to Assess and Build on Prior Knowledge in Mathematics (cont.)

## Think Sheet (cont.)

### Grades 1–2 Example

**Main Issue:** money

| My Questions | My Thoughts | Text Ideas |
|---|---|---|
| How many dimes in a dollar? | 100 | There are 10 dimes in a dollar. |
| How many pennies in 5 dimes? | 500 | There are 50 pennies in 5 dimes. |
| How many quarters in a dollar? | 4 | I was right! There are 4 quarters in a dollar. |

### Grades 3–5 Example

**Main Issue:** multiplication with multi-digit numbers: 3,671 x 3

| My Questions | My Thoughts | Text Ideas |
|---|---|---|
| Do I start with the 3 or the 1? | I think I start with the 1. | I am right! When multiplying a multi-digit number, the ones place is always first (in this problem, the 1). |
| 3 x 7 = 21. Do I write down 21? | I write only one number. | When the 3 is multiplied by the 7, I write down the 1 under the 7 and put the 2 above the hundreds place (the 6). |
| What do I do with the 2 above the 6? | Multiply it by 3, too. | First, I multiply the 6 by the 3 and then I add the 2 to the number. |

### Grades 6–8 Example

**Main Issue:** absolute value: $-|-4| - |9|$

| My Questions | My Thoughts | Text Ideas |
|---|---|---|
| Isn't everything positive with absolute values? | I think it depends on where the negatives are in the problem. | If the negative is placed within the absolute value bars, the number will be positive. In this problem, –4 becomes +4 and +9 stays +9. |
| What happens to the negative that is in front of the absolute value sign of the –4? | I see two negatives there and two negatives make a positive. | The first value is read as the opposite of the absolute value of –4. This means that the –4 becomes +4 within the absolute value signs and the opposite of +4 is –4, so the final value is –4. |

**Name:** _____

# Think Sheet

**Directions:** Write down the main topic of the reading. Next, write questions about the topic in the My Questions column. Write what you already know about the questions in the My Thoughts column. After reading, record important ideas in the Text Ideas column.

**Main Issue:** _____

| My Questions | My Thoughts | Text Ideas |
|---|---|---|
|  |  |  |
|  |  |  |
|  |  |  |
|  |  |  |
|  |  |  |
|  |  |  |

# Using Prediction and Inference in Mathematics

## Using Predictive Strategies

Closely related to assessing and building on prior knowledge is using predictive strategies to enhance reading comprehension. As the Report of the National Reading Panel (2000) has found in its analysis of reading research, prior knowledge affects a reader's comprehension by creating expectations about the content. This directs the reader's attention to the most important and relevant parts of the text, which enables the reader to infer from and elaborate on what is being read. As a result, the reader is able to fill in missing or incomplete information in the text. When drawing on prior knowledge and using prediction skills, the reader taps into the pre-existing mental structures, or schemata, to construct memory representations. Because these mental structures already exist, the reader is easily able to use, recall, and reconstruct the information in the text at a later time.

## What Is Prediction?

Making predictions can be described simply as the ability to guess what will happen and then read to see how things turn out. However, true predicting is not mere guesswork for successful readers. Readers rely heavily on their prior knowledge on a topic to determine their predictions. They use their prior knowledge to create a framework for understanding new material, and as they read, they determine whether or not their predictions were correct. We can call their predictions "educated guesses," but as Frank Smith (2004) asserts in *Understanding Reading: A Psycholinguistic Analysis of Reading and Learning to Read,* prediction simply means that the uncertainty of the reader is reduced to a few probable alternatives.

What makes good predictors good readers? Students who have encountered the information before, who are familiar with the story grammar, and who can guess the missing word are better readers. If the predictions are accurate, the process of reading is much more fluent, flexible, and effective.

## Prediction and Mathematics

Using predictive strategies is much like estimation and rounding in mathematics. Individuals examine the problem and the values it contains, and based on that examination, they will round the numbers up or down as needed, and then estimate, or predict an answer. This prediction gives the individual a general sense of the possible correct answer. Prediction in reading works in a similar way. Readers look at their reading material prior to reading; this is called previewing. This gives them clues about what to expect in the reading. Readers look at the title, the pictures, the organization, and the words chosen, and they compare and contrast what they see with what they already know. This enables them to predict the content of the selection. Predictions in reading direct readers' expectations about what they will find in the text.

# Using Prediction and Inference
# in Mathematics *(cont.)*

## Prediction and Mathematics *(cont.)*

We all make judgments about what we observe every day. We wake up, look out the window, and see that the sky is dark and cloudy, which usually indicates rain, so we decide to bring an umbrella along with us. We infer from the clouds and dark sky, based on our past experiences with these weather conditions, that it is likely to rain. We use inferential thinking when evaluating the information available to predict what will happen next. Math students use their observations to help them forecast, or make predictions, about problem outcomes.

## Making Inferences

Inferential thinking requires readers to read the text carefully, evaluate the information presented, and consider how it is presented in order to determine general facts or minute details, the author's purpose, and implications for and connections to other information. Students must use clues, references, and examples from the text to make inferences. They must also examine the connotative meanings of words used in the text to infer meaning.

## What the Research Says

While the connection between prediction and the activation of prior knowledge has been established by researchers, research conducted on prediction skills with informational texts is lacking. Reading researchers have focused on the effectiveness of prediction skills with narrative texts. Duke and Pearson (2002) demonstrate that engaging students in prediction behaviors has proven successful in increasing interest in and memory for stories. Duke

and Pearson (2002) point to Hansen's study (1981; Hansen and Pearson 1983), which shows that when students were encouraged to generate expectations about what characters might do based on their own experiences in similar situations, their reading comprehension was superior. They also performed better when reading similar stories independently. Duke and Pearson (2002) also point to the work of Neuman (1988) as demonstrating the power of prediction. When teachers presented students with oral previews of stories and turned these into discussions and predictions, story comprehension increased.

The Report of the National Reading Panel (2000) includes the following prediction activities as valuable procedures for improving reading comprehension: previewing the text by examining the structure, the visuals, the organization, and the content; answering pre-reading questions about the text in order to make predictions about the content based on the students' prior knowledge; searching the text and using what they know to answer inferential questions about the text; and encouraging students to compare their lives with situations in the text, either prior to or during the reading.

Developing prediction skills in students helps them set a purpose for reading, increases their motivation to read, instills curiosity, and heightens their motivation to learn (Ryder and Graves 2003).

# Strategies for Predicting and Inferring in Mathematics

## Picture Prediction

### Background Information

While many teachers work on prediction skills indirectly with students during story time, few extend the skill development during mathematics instruction. It is important to guide students to closely examine any pictures, tables, or graphs in a mathematics selection prior to reading in order to formulate some expectations about what they will learn. Students seem naturally drawn to the pictures in the textbook, but they need to develop inferential thinking so that they can more accurately predict the content of the reading. Teachers draw or gather images related and relevant to the reading selection to present to the students. After presenting the images, the teacher asks students to predict how the images are related to one another and to generate a list of words and concepts associated with the images. The students then try to anticipate the content of the reading selection because the better they are at anticipating the content, the more effective and fluent their reading comprehension is. As the students read the selection, they check to see how the images are related to the new information, allowing them to more efficiently incorporate new knowledge into their existing schema. Moreover, students are more motivated to read when they have determined their purpose in a reading task.

### Grade Levels/Standards Addressed

Grades 1–2 (Standard 5.2)
Grades 3–5 (Standards 5.1, 5.2)
Grades 6–8 (Standard 5.1)

### Activity

After carefully examining the reading selection, draw or gather three to six images directly related to and relevant to the content and arrange them in the desired order. Either place the images on the Picture Prediction sheet (page 92) and distribute them to small groups or individual students, or project the images on a large screen for the class to view. As students view the images, ask them to consider how the images are related to one another and predict the content of the reading. Place students in small groups, and ask them to generate a list of words or concepts associated with the pictures and the inferred topic of study. Have groups present their words and concepts as you write them on the board. Ask students to look over all of the words and try to generate any words that were not mentioned. As students tackle the reading selection, ask them to consider how the images are related to content and the new information they encounter. As an extended activity to encourage metacognitive skills, the students can write reflectively about their predictions and what they learned from the reading. They should consider the process as a whole.

### Differentiation

ELLs may have difficulty generating words related to the images, so it may help to have a list of words handy for them. To increase the challenge, the list might include words unrelated to the image in addition to words relevant to the topic of study. Students reading below grade level will work best in the small-group setting. Gifted students will enjoy the challenge of the activity, particularly if they have a different set of images related to the topic of study to work with.

# Strategies for Predicting and Inferring in Mathematics (cont.)

## Picture Prediction (cont.)

### Grades 1–2 Example

**Directions:** Write down any words that you think of when you look at the pictures. Think about what you will be reading, and write down what you think the reading will be about.

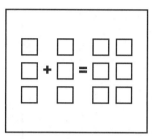 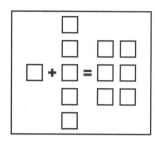 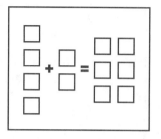

**Words**
six, plus, equals, two, three, five, one, four, add

**My Prediction**
The examples are about the numbers that can add up to six.

### Grades 3–5 Example

**Directions:** Write down any words that you think of when you look at the pictures. Think about what you will be reading, and write down what you think the reading will be about.

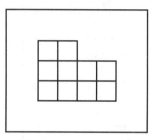 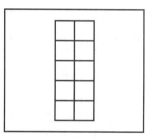 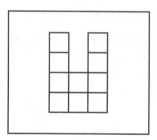

**Words**
square units, area, figure, count, ten, equal

**My Prediction**
The examples are about area. Each figure has the same number of square units, and therefore the same area.

### Grades 6–8 Example

**Directions:** Write down any words that you think of when you look at the pictures. Think about what you will be reading, and write down what you think the reading will be about.

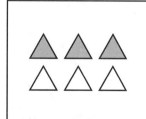 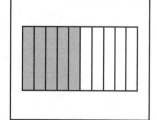 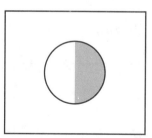

**Words**
one-half, decimal, percentage, fraction

**My Prediction**
We are going to be learning how to convert fractions to decimals and decimals to percentages.

# Picture Prediction

**Directions:** Write down any words that you think of when you look at the pictures. Think about what you will be reading, and write down what you think the reading will be about.

**Words**

_____

_____

**My Prediction**

_____

_____

# Strategies for Predicting and Inferring in Mathematics *(cont.)*

## Text and Subtext

### Background Information

When students make inferences while reading, they make connections to what they already know, to other information they have read, and to their general knowledge of the world around them. They take what they "see" and infer information that is not directly stated in the reading. Students are generally taught inferential reasoning when reading fiction, but teachers should also extend the skill practice to nonfiction materials (Hoyt 2002). It is essential to guide students in their development of inferential thinking skills when working with nonfiction and informational reading materials in mathematics because students need to learn how to make inferences about the real world around them. As Hoyt (2002) points out, "With adequate modeling, readers can infer from even so little as a sentence and experience the power of reading beyond what is stated."

Teachers can begin the explicit instruction of inferential reasoning by allowing students to interpret body language, facial expressions, pictures in reading books, photographs, and short predictable stories. After much practice, students can extrapolate information from the text to demonstrate insight on the topic of study.

### Grade Levels/Standards Addressed

Grades 3–5 (Standard 5.3)
Grades 6–8 (Standard 7.5)

### Activity

Begin the activity with teacher modeling and demonstration. Conduct a read aloud of the mathematics reading selection for the students. When finished, locate a quote from which students can infer and interpret its meaning. Write the quote on the board and ask students to write it on their Text and Subtext graphic organizers (page 95). Model for the students how to restate the information from the text in their own words by thinking aloud and writing your thoughts on the board. Ask the students to study the two statements, and then explain what information they can infer. The students should look at word choice, sentence structure, and details. When the students use inference, they are also identifying the subtext. Guide students in using their inferring skills to identify the subtext. After students identify the subtext, hold a class discussion to further explore meaning and implications of the subtext.

### Differentiation

Teaching inference can be tricky, so it is best to provide individual instruction for both ELLs and students reading below grade level. All students will benefit from heterogeneous grouping for this activity. It is important for ELLs to have adequate modeling for this activity. Make sure that the reading selection is at an appropriate level for students reading below grade level. Gifted students may need little instruction and may prefer to work independently.

# Strategies for Predicting and Inferring in Mathematics *(cont.)*

## Text and Subtext *(cont.)*

### Grades 3–5 Example

**Directions:** After completing the reading, work with your teacher to find a quote from which you can infer meaning. Then restate the information from the quote in your own words. Using the two sentences, along with your inferring skills, write the subtext.

**Restate the reading selection in your own words**

When doing division, it is possible to check answers by using multiplication. When doing multiplication, it is possible to check answers by using division.

**Quote from the reading**

"The inverse relationship of multiplication and division can be used to check answers."

**Subtext**

Knowing the fact families for multiplication and division makes checking answers easier.

### Grades 6–8 Example

**Directions:** After completing the reading, work with your teacher to find a quote from which you can infer meaning. Then restate the information from the quote in your own words. Using the two sentences, along with your inferring skills, write the subtext.

**Restate the reading selection in your own words**

Janet must calculate the cost of 25 students at $6.50 per person and then add $20.00 for renting the lanes.

**Quote from the reading**

"Each game of bowling costs $6.50 per person, and it costs $20.00 to rent the 5 lanes in the bowling alley for Janet's class of 25 students."

**Subtext**

The linear equation would be:
Total Cost = $6.50 (number of people) + $20.00 or $y = 6.5x + 20$.

**Name:** _____

# Text and Subtext

**Directions:** After completing the reading, work with your teacher to find a quote from which you can infer meaning. Then restate the information from the quote in your own words. Using the two sentences, along with your inferring skills, write the subtext.

## Restate the reading selection in your own words

_____

_____

_____

_____

## Quote from the reading

_____

_____

_____

_____

## Subtext

_____

_____

_____

_____

# Strategies for Predicting and Inferring in Mathematics *(cont.)*

## Anticipation Guide

### Background Information

An effective way to increase interest, develop motivation, and engage students in a mathematics reading task is to provide them with an Anticipation Guide. Initially, Anticipation Guides may seem like a test to students, but they resemble the fun magazine quizzes that students enjoy taking. The goal is to draw on students' prior knowledge and relate the knowledge to the reading content.

### Grade Levels/Standards Addressed

Grades 1–2 (Standard 5.2)
Grades 3–5 (Standard 5.3)
Grades 6–8 (Standard 5.1)

### Preparation

The guidelines for constructing an Anticipation Guide (Vacca and Vacca 2005) are as follows:

1. Analyze the material to be read. Determine the most important ideas—implicit and explicit—for consideration.

2. Write the major ideas in short, clear, declarative, and thought-provoking statements. These statements should enable students to connect with the ideas personally. Avoid abstractions and narrow statements that focus on details or factual information.

3. Put these statements in a format that will elicit anticipation and prediction. This can be challenging because some topics can seem to be dry and uninteresting. Write the statements so that they generate strong feelings in the reader. Limit the number of statements to five or six in order to maintain the focus on the learning objectives.

### Activity

After distributing the prepared Anticipation Guide (page 99), ask students to respond to the statements individually. Discuss their responses either as a class or in small groups, so students have an opportunity to talk about their ideas at length. Ask probing questions and challenge students' ideas, but remain open to a wide range of responses. As students read the assigned selection, tell them to contrast their predictions with the author's intended meaning. After the students complete the reading, ask them to consider what they just learned in contrast to their initial opinions. The activity can be extended by having the students write reflectively about their initial attitudes and about how the discussion and reading altered or reaffirmed their attitudes toward the ideas.

### Variation

With primary students, make a list of true and false statements based on the reading. Place the statements on the board or on a poster. Allow students to take the quiz, and tally the number of students who vote true and false for each statement. As they listen to a read-aloud, they can check their answers against the information presented.

### Differentiation

ELLs and students reading below grade level should be provided with a vocabulary list of key terms to help them understand the statements on the Anticipation Guide. Read the statements aloud as the students complete the guides and explain the meaning of the statements using other phrases and terms. Ask gifted students to write a summary of what they expect to find in the reading before the reading task has been assigned.

# Strategies for Predicting and Inferring in Mathematics *(cont.)*

## Anticipation Guide *(cont.)*

### Grades 1–2 Example

**Directions:** Carefully read the statements below. Think about each statement. Decide if you think it is true or false. Mark an *X* on the line for your answer.

**Topic: <u>Fractions</u>**

True      False

\_\_\_\_\_ \_\_\_\_\_   $\frac{1}{2}$ is more than $\frac{1}{4}$

\_\_\_\_\_ \_\_\_\_\_   $\frac{1}{3}$ is less than $\frac{1}{2}$

\_\_\_\_\_ \_\_\_\_\_   $\frac{1}{5}$ is equal to $\frac{1}{5}$

\_\_\_\_\_ \_\_\_\_\_   $\frac{4}{4}$ is more than $\frac{2}{4}$

### Grades 3–5 Example

**Directions:** Carefully read the statements below. Think about each statement and determine if you generally agree or disagree with it by marking an *X* next to your answer. Be sure to provide an explanation for your response by writing it on the line next to "Why?"

**Topic: <u>Integers and Inequalities</u>**

1. $0 < -2$
   Agree \_\_\_\_ Disagree \_\_\_\_ Why? _____

2. $-4 > -1$
   Agree \_\_\_\_ Disagree \_\_\_\_ Why? _____

3. $7 < -8$
   Agree \_\_\_\_ Disagree \_\_\_\_ Why? _____

4. $9 > -1$
   Agree \_\_\_\_ Disagree \_\_\_\_ Why? _____

5. $-4 < -4$
   Agree \_\_\_\_ Disagree \_\_\_\_ Why? _____

# Strategies for Predicting and Inferring in Mathematics *(cont.)*

## Anticipation Guide *(cont.)*

### Grades 6–8 Example

**Directions:** Carefully read the statements below. Think about each statement and determine if you generally agree or disagree with it by marking an X next to your answer. Be sure to provide an explanation for your response by writing it on the line next to "Why?"

**Topic: <u>Linear Functions: $4y = 8x + 16$</u>**

1.  If $x = 0$, then $y = 4$.
    Agree _____  Disagree _____  Why? _____

2.  If $y = 0$, then $x = 16$.
    Agree _____  Disagree _____  Why? _____

3.  The slope of the equation is 8.
    Agree _____  Disagree _____  Why? _____

4.  The $b$ value, or constant, is 4.
    Agree _____  Disagree _____  Why? _____

5.  The graph of this equation would move upward in direction.
    Agree _____  Disagree _____  Why? _____

**Name:** _____

# Anticipation Guide

**Directions:** Carefully read the statements below. Think about each statement and determine if you generally agree or disagree with it by marking an X next to your answer. Be sure to provide an explanation for your response by writing it on the line next to "Why?"

**Topic:** _____

1. _____
   _____

   Agree _____ Disagree _____ Why? _____
   _____

2. _____
   _____

   Agree _____ Disagree _____ Why? _____
   _____
   _____

3. _____
   _____

   Agree _____ Disagree _____ Why? _____
   _____

4. _____
   _____

   Agree _____ Disagree _____ Why? _____
   _____

5. _____
   _____

   Agree _____ Disagree _____ Why? _____
   _____

# Strategies for Predicting and Inferring in Mathematics (cont.)

## Wordsplash

## Background Information

Wordsplash is a vocabulary activity created by W. Dorsey Hammond, a professor of education at Salisbury University. Wordsplash generates interest on a topic, draws on students' prior knowledge, and asks them to make predictions about how words are related to each other and to the topic. Prior to assigning a mathematics reading task, the teacher selects words and concepts from the article or text. The words should be placed randomly on a page. The students then examine the words and work either individually or in a group to predict the relationships between the words and the topic being studied. The students write down statements in which they explain the relationships. Once the statements are generated, the students read the text and check the accuracy of their predictions. The activity increases comprehension because the students spend time anticipating what they will encounter in the reading material. Wordsplash allows the students to see that they already know something about the topic being studied. Even if the students' predictions are inaccurate, they establish a framework for learning new information from the reading by making a personal connection to it.

### Grade Levels/Standards Addressed

Grades 3–5 (Standard 5.3)
Grades 6–8 (Standard 5.1)

## Activity

After carefully reading the text, select key words and important concepts from the article or text. Limit the number of words to no more than ten. Next prepare a Wordsplash activity sheet (page 102) in which the words appear randomly on the page. Place students in groups or direct them to work individually to write a short paragraph that explains how the words and concepts work together. After the students have finished writing, hold a brief discussion about their predictions. Then allow students to read the text to see if their predictions were accurate. Prompt them to compare and contrast their paragraphs with the material in the reading. Have the students share their predictions and findings with the class. Extend the activity by asking the students to write a reflective paragraph about the process.

## Differentiation

If some words on the Wordsplash activity sheet are not easily understood by ELLs or students reading below grade level, be sure to provide definitions for them. Read the words aloud to the students and provide visuals if possible to aid in their understanding of the vocabulary. Gifted students should be encouraged to add additional words to the Wordsplash activity and identify those words for the class.

# Strategies for Predicting and Inferring in Mathematics (cont.)

## Wordsplash (cont.)

### Grades 3–5 Example

**Directions:** After examining the words below, write a few sentences or a paragraph using the words.

| | | |
|---|---|---|
| rectangle | pentagon | hexagon |
| octagon | | sides |
| | triangle | corner |
| right angle | parallelogram | |

**Wordsplash summary**

Different shapes have a certain number of sides and corners. A rectangle has four sides and four corners. A pentagon has five sides and five corners. A hexagon has six sides and six corners. An octagon has eight sides and eight corners. A triangle has three sides and three corners. Some shapes also have right angles. A rectangle has four right angles, which means the angles are 90°. A parallelogram has sides that are parallel. A rectangle is a parallelogram.

### Grades 6–8 Example

**Directions:** After examining the words below, write a few sentences or a paragraph using the words.

| | | |
|---|---|---|
| variable | variable expression | symbol |
| | | coefficient |
| equation | | inequality |
| evaluate | constant | |
| | | numerical expression |

**Wordsplash summary**

A variable is any symbol that is used in place of a number. A variable expression is an expression that includes a variable in it. A numerical expression is a value that contains only numbers and no variables. An equation is grouping variable or numerical expressions together using an equals sign. A coefficient is a number that is in front of a variable. A constant is a value, or number, within an equation that does not contain a variable. To evaluate an equation or expression means to find the numerical value, or answer, that is being represented.

# Wordsplash

**Directions:** After examining the words below, write a few sentences or a paragraph using the words.

**Wordsplash summary**

_____

_____

_____

_____

# Strategies for Predicting and Inferring in Mathematics *(cont.)*

## Preview

### Background Information

An effective pre-reading activity that prepares students for reading is a Preview. As the name implies, Previews are short summaries—usually five to ten minutes long—that the teacher reads aloud to the students before the students begin a reading task. Students can read Previews silently, but research shows that they are more effective when read aloud and followed by a discussion with predicting activities (Neuman 1988, as cited by Duke and Pearson 2002). By providing students with a Preview, teachers activate and build on students' background knowledge, establish a purpose for reading, and give students the opportunity to discuss or question information prior to reading (Ryder and Graves 2003). The best Previews connect the mathematics material to the students' lives and experiences, provide students with an overall summary, establish a context and purpose for the reading task, and ask questions that stimulate thinking. This strategy stimulates curiosity and increases students' motivation to read. Rather than ruin the reading experience, Previews, if written correctly, help students understand the reading material and orient their thinking on the topic of study.

### Grade Levels/Standards Addressed

Grades 1–2 (Standard 7.2)
Grades 3–5 (Standard 7.6)
Grades 6–8 (Standard 7.4)

### Preparation

Ryder and Graves (2003) suggest the following steps when constructing the Preview. Carefully review the reading material and establish the learning objectives. Note the important concepts, people, and events, and define the main ideas. When constructing the introductory statement, consider how to make the information relevant and useful to students. End the introduction with a question that draws on students' prior knowledge. Next write a summary that includes the main ideas and supporting details in the order they appear in the reading. Emphasize the information in the beginning of the reading, and do not give away any resolution or conclusions. In the end, construct purpose-setting questions that stimulate interest in the topic.

### Activity

When presenting the Preview to the students, familiarize yourself with what you have written so that the presentation is fluid and interesting. Inform the students that you are about to introduce a section of reading to them and begin the Preview. Point out other things, such as illustrations or experiments, that students should consider as they read to help them comprehend the material.

### Differentiation

Speak slowly and clearly; use intonation, volume, and pauses; rephrase statements and questions; and repeat key concepts to help ELLs understand better. Carefully assess the prior knowledge of students reading below grade level so that you can more effectively construct the preview to link to their background knowledge and prior experiences. Ask gifted students open-ended questions to be explored through further independent research or reading.

# Strategies for Predicting and Inferring in Mathematics *(cont.)*

## Preview *(cont.)*

### Grades 1–2 Example

We are about to learn how to subtract numbers. How many of you have heard the word *subtract*? We have already learned what it means to add, right? Can anyone explain what we are doing when we add numbers?

Well, instead of putting numbers together, with subtraction, we start with one number and take away another number. You will probably hear me use the words *take away* instead of *subtract*.

If we have two numbers like 10 and 4, which number do you think we would start with? Do you think we would start with 10 and take away 4? Can we start with 4 and take away 10? What if the numbers were candies? Would you start with 10 candies and take away, or eat, 4, or would you start with 4 candies and take away, or eat, 10?

### Grades 3–5 Example

We are going to be learning how to figure out how much things cost when you go shopping. How many of you would like to be able to go to the store and buy $100 worth of video games? What if I told you that you could go to the store and buy 5 video games for $100? Does anyone know how to find out the cost of each game?

Well, if you can get 5 games for $100, then you just have to divide the $100 by 5. Does anyone know the answer? That is right—$20. Not only can we find out the unit cost of each game, but we can also find out how many video games we can buy with a given amount of money.

We now know that our video games are $20 each, right? How many video games could you buy with $300? What about $350?

### Grades 6–8 Example

How many of you like a good sale on the newest pair of shoes? Well, it is important to know how to calculate percent increases and decreases when you go shopping. Imagine you have $100 to buy this new pair of shoes that you really want. Normally, the shoes are $125, but today, they are 30% off. Do you have enough money? What about tax? How much is tax?

Let's figure it out. How do you find 30% of 125? You must convert the percentage value into a decimal. Start by multiplying $125 by 0.3. That comes to $37.50. Does that mean that the shoes are $37.50? No—that is the amount of the discount that you get on the shoes. So what is the cost of the shoes with the discount? Well, $125 – $37.50 is $87.50. So if you have a $100, you can buy them right? Not so fast!

Tax is 8.25%. Now you have to take the $87.50 and find out how much money the state wants to collect on the purchase of your shoes. $87.50 times .0825 (8.25% converted to a decimal) is $7.21875, which the government will round up to $7.22. Now you must add the cost of your shoes ($87.50) and the state tax ($7.22) for a grand total of $94.72. Do you have enough money? Just barely! What if the shoes were originally $135—is $100 enough? What if the shoes were $150, but the discount was 40%?

# Think-Alouds and Comprehension-Monitoring in Mathematics

## Metacognitive Thinking

The knowledge of and control over one's ability to think and learn is referred to as *metacognition*. In other words, metacognition is thinking about thinking. To be metacognitive is to be able to reflect on one's own thinking processes; it includes knowing about oneself as a learner, about the tasks one attempts, and about the techniques one uses to understand the world, reading material, and oneself. Researchers include in the definition of metacognition the word *control* because self-awareness also includes self-monitoring and regulating of one's thinking. Readers use metacognition to plan how they will read, to predict what will happen in the reading, to check for accuracy in their predictions, to monitor their comprehension, to evaluate their progress, to remediate when difficulties arise, and to revise their strategies for learning when necessary (Baker 2002).

It is well accepted in the reading research community that metacognition plays an important role in reading comprehension. Furthermore, metacognition is firmly established in theories of reading and learning. Reading researchers have long acknowledged that highly skilled readers monitor their comprehension while they are reading (Block and Pressley 2003). Good readers are aware of the thinking processes involved in reading. They establish a goal or purpose before they read, and they can adjust their goal while reading. They reflect on the author's purpose before, during, and after reading. Essentially, good readers can identify the elements of a passage that are confusing, and they can select a strategy to figure out what they do not understand. Most importantly, they can talk about what it is they are doing as they read.

Poor readers do not have such self-awareness as they read, and as a result they have difficulty articulating their thought processes. They have trouble identifying the source of their struggle. Research demonstrates that they cannot become proficient unless their teachers can demonstrate and model for them how to think while they are reading (Block and Israel 2004). This process comes naturally to English or language arts teachers, but mathematics teachers may not be aware of the benefits of teaching using think-alouds and comprehension monitoring techniques when working with informational texts in mathematics.

Based on the research it has reviewed, the National Reading Panel (2000) concludes that metacognition and comprehension monitoring should be fostered in comprehension instruction. Therefore, children must have opportunities to develop and enhance metacognitive skills to meet the demands of understanding print material. Numerous studies provide solid evidence that comprehension monitoring skills of good and poor readers alike can be enhanced through direct instruction. The development of metacognitive skills in students should begin with direct teacher explanations and modeling of reading comprehension strategies, but it develops more fully when students practice using comprehension strategies as they read (Pressley 2002a). Pressley (2002a) points out that it is especially helpful if students can practice and are given opportunities to explain how they use the strategies and reflect on the use of these strategies over the course of a semester.

# Think-Alouds and Comprehension-Monitoring in Mathematics *(cont.)*

## What Is a Think-Aloud?

Think-alouds, also known as mental modeling (Ryder and Graves 2003), are strategies to verbalize a teacher's thoughts aloud to students while reading a selection orally. As the teachers talk about their thoughts, they model the process of comprehension for the students and can focus on the reasoning involved while reading. Think-alouds allow readers to stop periodically to reflect on the thinking they do to understand a text and then relate these processes orally for the benefit of the listeners. Teachers use this technique to help students verbalize their thoughts while reading so that they can duplicate the process later when reading independently. Research demonstrates that the metacognitive awareness involved in think-aloud strategies significantly increases students' scores on comprehension tests, adds to the students' ability for comprehension monitoring, and improves students' skills in selecting fix-up strategies to overcome comprehension struggles while they read (Block and Israel 2004).

Think-alouds are used in conjunction with other reading comprehension strategies during instruction. Teachers should employ think-alouds as they model how to use a reading comprehension strategy at appropriate points in the reading process. Think-alouds differ from explanation because they occur when the teacher is actually using a reading comprehension strategy while reading. Modeling is a much more effective method for teaching reasoning than explanation because the strategy use is much clearer to students.

The think-aloud is a teaching technique that comes easily to teachers who are metacognitive themselves in that they are very aware of their own thinking processes as they read. One of the characteristics of highly effective comprehension teachers is their own understanding of their metacognitive thinking. Skilled comprehension teachers take the time to understand their thoughts as they read. As they read, they scrutinize the reading materials, record what ideas come to mind, pay attention to which areas may cause confusion, consider which fix-up strategies they can use, develop questions and answers about what they are reading, and summarize the content in a variety of ways, among a number of other activities. Obviously, teachers who involve their own metacognitive thinking as they develop lessons are doing a tremendous amount of work. One of the reasons teachers do not teach think-aloud strategies is because they feel it is difficult to do (Block and Israel 2004; Baker 2002).

While teaching students to become more aware of their understanding while reading, the goal is to go beyond teaching students how to think about their thinking. Metacognition should not be promoted as a goal in itself, taught in isolation, but rather as a tool that is integrated with comprehension instruction (Baker 2002).

Traditionally, there has been a tendency among educators to focus on word recognition and vocabulary development in the primary grades and focus on comprehension skills in the upper grades. As Michael Pressley (2002b) points out, this view has been increasingly rejected in favor of developing comprehension skills during the primary grades with the expectation that such instruction will hopefully affect children dramatically in the short term and lead to the development of better comprehension skills over the long term.

# Think-Alouds and Comprehension-Monitoring in Mathematics (cont.)

## How to Construct a Think-Aloud

The steps for developing think-alouds are as follows (Readence, Bean, and Baldwin 2000):

- Select a short passage. The passage should be somewhat difficult so that when you explain your thinking and reasoning, it will make sense and be useful to the students. If the passage is too easy, the students will lose interest.

- Think about the comments you can make for the think-aloud based on the students' experiences. Since the material is not difficult for you, you need to prepare the think-aloud to model the metacognitive skills that will benefit the students.

- Prior to beginning the think-aloud, explain to the students what you will be doing. Be explicit so that they know what to expect and what they should be learning from listening to you.

- As you read the passage to the students, pause and insert your comments as necessary. Pause after you make each comment so that students have enough time to process your thinking strategies. It may be difficult for them to follow another person's train of thought, so allow adequate time for processing.

- When you are finished, encourage the students to ask you questions about how you think or about the think-aloud strategy.

## Think-Aloud Activities

The think-aloud activities come directly from those presented in Cathy Collins Block and Susan Israel's *The ABCs of Performing Highly Effective Think-Alouds* except for the Determine Word Meanings Think-Aloud.

## Monitoring Comprehension

An important part of comprehension instruction is teaching readers the importance of monitoring their understanding of what they are reading and helping them develop the tools to do so (Neufeld 2005). However, Neufeld (2005) points out that teaching students how to monitor their understanding is only part of the process. Students must be able to figure out what to do (which strategy to use) when they have a comprehension breakdown. Students should be able to ask themselves questions to check their own understanding. Examples of questions include: *Do I understand what I just read? What parts were confusing or unclear?* In addition, students should be able to ask and answer journalistic-type questions as they monitor their own understanding of text. Questions of this type might include *who, what, where, when, why,* and *how* questions. Readers should be able to generate a summary of a text as a way to monitor their own comprehension, and if they struggle to write a summary, this is a clear sign that there is a comprehension breakdown.

# Think-Alouds and Comprehension-Monitoring in Mathematics *(cont.)*

## Monitoring Comprehension *(cont.)*

Proficient readers act in the following ways as they monitor their reading for meaning (Keene 2002):

- Know when text makes sense, when it does not, what does not make sense, and whether the unclear portions are critical to their overall understanding of the piece.

- Identify when text is comprehensible and recognize the degree to which they are understanding it. Identify ways in which a text becomes gradually more understandable by reading past an unclear portion or by rereading parts of the whole text.

- Are aware of the processes readers can use to make meaning clear. Check, evaluate, and revise the evolving interpretation of the text while reading.

- Identify confusing ideas, themes, or surface elements (words, sentence or text structures, graphs, tables, and so on) and can suggest a variety of different means to solve the problems readers may encounter.

- Are aware of what they need to comprehend in relation to the purpose for reading.

- Learn how to pause, consider the meanings in text, reflect on understandings, and use different strategies to enhance understanding. Readers best learn this process by watching proficient models think aloud and by gradually taking responsibility for monitoring their own comprehension as they read independently.

# Think-Alouds and Comprehension-Monitoring in Mathematics *(cont.)*

## Fix-up Strategies

When students begin to understand the nature of their comprehension breakdown, they must determine what kind of clarification they need and use a fix-up strategy to solve the problem. When readers struggle through a section of text, they must evaluate the strategies they know to determine which one will work best to understand the text. They also must determine whether it is necessary to completely understand the portion of the text that is causing them trouble. Fix-up strategies used by the most expert readers include rereading parts or all of the text, scanning or looking ahead to preview information, pausing and connecting information to what the reader already knows, examining other resources on the same topic, and seeking support from more knowledgeable readers (Neufeld 2005). In addition, proficient readers use the six major systems of language (graphophonic, lexical, syntactic, semantic, schematic, and pragmatic) to solve reading problems (Keene 2002). They ask the following questions when they are not comprehending:

- Does this word, phrase, sentence, or passage make sense?

- Does the word I'm pronouncing sound like language?

- Do the letters in the word match the sounds I'm pronouncing?

- Have I seen this word before?

- Do the pictures give me a clue about what the sentence says?

- Is there another reader who can help me make sense of this?

- What do I already know from my experience and the context of this text that can help me solve this problem?

- How can I find the main idea?

- How can I figure out what the words imply?

Keene (2002) also asserts that proficient readers know a wide range of problem-solving strategies and can make appropriate choices in a given reading situation (that is, skip ahead or reread, use the context and syntax, sound it out, speak to another reader, consider relevant prior knowledge, read the passage aloud, and so on).

# Think-Alouds and Comprehension-Monitoring Strategies for Mathematics

## Overview the Text Think-Aloud

### Background Information

Block and Israel (2004) note the importance of modeling what expert readers think before they read a large section of text. The Overview the Text Think-Aloud (Block and Israel 2004) uses mental modeling for students to demonstrate connections that readers make prior to actually reading and shows how to activate prior knowledge on a given topic. Teachers need to model for students how to examine the pictures, writing style, organization, genre characteristics, and other qualities in order to preview the text prior to reading because these actions improve comprehension.

---

### Grade Levels/Standards Addressed

Grades 1–2 (Standard 5.7)
Grades 3–5 (Standard 5.8)
Grades 6–8 (Standard 5.4)

---

### Activity

Present a selection of text (e.g., textbook page, activity page, workbook page, biography). Describe to students what attracted you to it, how you knew you would like the topic, how many times you have read something on the same topic, etc. Explain the use of visuals, diagrams, examples, pictures, headings, level of vocabulary, organization, etc., that can help you understand the text. Hold up the text and say:

**Grades 1–2** *Let's look at this text (textbook page, activity page, etc.). I wonder what it is going to be about. I can read the title. I've read other things about this topic before. I want to know if I can read all the words on this page. I can look quickly over the page to find any words I don't recognize. There might be boldfaced words that are important to know. I see a picture and a graph on this page. Pictures and graphs can help me understand the text. Let me see. I think this book is going to be about…*

**Grades 3–5** *Before you start reading something new, carefully take a look at the text. Think about the topic and how much you want to learn or do. Read the title and any boldfaced headings. Think about the last time you read about the same subject. Look over the text to see if you can understand all of the words. Decide if the text has pictures, numbered steps, boldfaced words, or graphs that can help you. Sometimes important information is in a box or in the margin. Use what you find to guess what the text is about.*

# Think-Alouds and Comprehension-Monitoring Strategies for Mathematics *(cont.)*

## Overview the Text Think-Aloud *(cont.)*

### Activity *(cont.)*

**Grades 6–8** *The first time you look at something to read, consider how much you want to learn about a topic. Read the headings and examples to see if you have come across similar material before. Skim the page to see if it contains too many difficult words for you to understand. Also, decide if the reading has too few pictures or too little information. Check over the table of contents, activities, key words, and diagrams. Try to predict what will be covered in the selection (Block and Israel 2004, 155).*

Finish the think-aloud by reminding students that they will begin to develop the skill to automatically complete an effective overview every time they choose a book, which will help them understand and enjoy their reading more.

### Differentiation

Use the reading material as a concrete example for ELLs. It is best to have the first reading selection on an overhead so that you can point to different sections. Repeat and rephrase key concepts and key vocabulary for ELLs as you think aloud. Be sure to show students reading below grade level how to identify the table of contents, headings, and subheadings. Use visual cues, as they may not be familiar with the organizing features of the text. Gifted students should be invited to share their thinking with the class and explain their thinking processes as much as possible.

# Think-Alouds and Comprehension-Monitoring Strategies for Mathematics *(cont.)*

## Preparing for the Topic Think-Aloud

### Background Information

Block and Israel (2004) express the need for students to learn how to think about a topic prior to reading. It is important for teachers and proficient readers to model for students how to think about the purpose and main ideas as they begin to read a selection for the first time. Closely examining the first few paragraphs increases students' comprehension because they can more rapidly identify the types of details that will reappear in a book. They can also predict more reliably how main ideas and detail sentences will be connected and what meaning will be revealed in later detail sentences.

> ### Grade Levels/Standards Addressed
>
> Grades 1–2 (Standard 5.7)
> Grades 3–5 (Standard 5.8)
> Grades 6–8 (Standard 5.4)

### Activity

Tell students that when they begin reading in mathematics, they should think about the purpose and main ideas and pay particular attention to all details in the first few sentences. Explain that these pieces of information are used to help the reader decide to continue reading (or listening). Tell students to familiarize themselves with the author's train of thought during the first few sentences, so they can align their thinking in the same direction. Before the students begin reading, hold up the mathematics book and say:

*When I begin to read nonfiction, I read the first few sentences to put details together, identify where the author puts his or her main ideas, and find out what kinds of details this writer uses to describe a main point. By thinking these thoughts, I can more quickly follow the author's train of thought (Block and Israel 2004, 156).*

Afterwards, read a bit more of the text. Describe how you identify those sentences that are main idea statements and what kinds of details the author uses. Tell students that most authors put the most important, or main idea, statement either as the first or last sentence in a paragraph. If it is the first sentence, it usually introduces the topic of that paragraph and all remaining sentences describe something about that topic. If it is the last sentence, it usually ties all the details in the prior sentences together and is a more general summary statement.

Inform the students that detail statements answer the *how*, *why*, *when*, *where*, *who*, or *what* questions. Tell the students that most books rely on only one type of detail statement to move the sequence of ideas forward. By reading the first few paragraphs, students can determine which type of detail statement will be used in that selection or lesson.

# Think-Alouds and Comprehension-Monitoring Strategies for Mathematics *(cont.)*

## Preparing for the Topic Think-Aloud *(cont.)*

### Activity *(cont.)*

Next, repeat the Preparing for the Topic Think-Aloud with a different reading selection or lesson on the same topic to demonstrate how to begin thinking about the topic and the author's train of thought within the first few sentences. Discuss how different authors have different styles and patterns of writing about the same subject. Go into great depth in the examination of the detail statements. Finally, ask the students to describe their thought processes as they read the opening of another nonfiction selection or lesson.

### Differentiation

Use the reading material as a concrete example for ELLs. It is best to have the first reading selection on an overhead so that it can be referred to. Repeat and rephrase key concepts and key vocabulary for ELLs as you think aloud. Invite and encourage students reading below grade level and the rest of the class to share all of their thinking—even their struggling, negative thoughts—by modeling this for them. Invite gifted students to share their thinking with the class and explain their processes as much as possible, particularly when they run into difficulties.

# Think-Alouds and Comprehension-Monitoring Strategies for Mathematics (cont.)

## Look for Important Information Think-Aloud

### Background Information

Block and Israel (2004) note that expert readers know how to pay greater attention to important sentences, and they know how to ignore the minor details that may distract them from their goals. They present the following activity to assist students in learning how to locate the most important information in a reading selection after watching the process modeled by their teacher.

### Grade Levels/Standards Addressed

Grades 1–2 (Standard 5.7)
Grades 3–5 (Standard 5.8)
Grades 6–8 (Standard 5.4)

### Activity

Hold up a mathematics textbook and turn to a chapter students have not yet read. Say aloud:

**Grades 1–2** *At the beginning of a reading selection, the author usually tells you how to find the most important information. The author says certain words more than once. Sometimes the author says the same thing more than once. Sometimes the author gives examples. If you can find the author's big idea, then you can find the most important information faster. Notice how the most important thing to learn is right here (point to a sentence that contains a key idea and describe how you know it is important).*

**Grades 3–5** *At the beginning of a chapter or a book, the author gives clues to help you find the most important information. The author repeats important words and restates important ideas more often than others. The most important idea is usually followed by certain phrases such as* for example, for instance, *or* to illustrate. *Also, when you know where the author generally puts the main ideas in the paragraphs, it is much easier to find the most important points. For example, in this section, the author's most important points appear here in this paragraph (point to a sentence containing a key idea and describe how you know it is important).*

**Grades 6–8** *At the beginning of a chapter or book, the author reveals clues to help you locate and understand the most important information. The author repeats certain words and restates some ideas more frequently than others. Another clue is that the most important idea is often followed by a sentence that gives an example or contains the words* for example, for instance, *or* to illustrate. *Also, when you identify where the author places the main ideas in paragraphs, you can find the most important points more quickly. For instance, in this reading selection the author's most important points appear here in this paragraph (point to a sentence containing a key idea and describe how you know it is important) (Block and Israel 2004, 157).*

# Think-Alouds and Comprehension-Monitoring Strategies for Mathematics (cont.)

## Look for Important Information Think-Aloud (cont.)

### Activity (cont.)

Ask the students to follow along as you read the next paragraph. Have them work in pairs to identify the clues that point out the most important idea or sentence in that paragraph. Continue asking the students to perform Look for Important Information Think-Alouds as a whole group, in small groups, in pairs, and individually until the class can do it independently. Monitor the students individually as they read silently.

### Differentiation

Place the key phrases *for example, for instance, such as,* and *to illustrate* on the board to help ELLs identify them while reading. Make sure to rephrase and repeat key concepts and words for ELLs. Students reading below grade level will benefit from having the selection placed on an overhead transparency so that they can follow the instructions very closely. It may be necessary to provide gifted students who are expert readers with a more challenging reading selection.

# Think-Alouds and Comprehension-Monitoring Strategies for Mathematics (cont.)

## Activate Prior Knowledge Think-Aloud

### Background Information

As reading researchers assert, the best readers activate their prior knowledge and background experiences prior to reading (Duke and Pearson 2002). In doing so, they make it possible for new information that they encounter to be organized in an accessible locale within their schemata. Struggling readers need guidance and modeling via the think-aloud technique so that they can see how expert readers make connections between what they already know and what they are learning. This technique teaches them how to make connections when they are reading independently.

### Grade Levels/Standards Addressed

Grades 1–2 (Standard 5.7, 7.4)
Grades 3–5 (Standards 5.8, 7.6)
Grades 6–8 (Standard 5.4, 7.4)

### Activity

Select a section of text for students to read. After they have read about four pages, interrupt students. Say:

**Grades 1–2** *When you listen to someone read or when you read by yourself, you can think about what you know about the topic. What things have you heard about the topic? What have you done or seen that is related to the topic? You could stop paying attention, but you might miss something important. Good readers pay close attention to what is being read. They stop and they think about what they know about the topic. They think about what they have seen or done in their own lives. I am going to show you how I think about what I know as we continue to read the next page.*

**Grades 3–5** *After reading the first few pages of any reading material, you can continue to read carefully and think about things you have learned or experiences you have had that are very similar to the information in the reading. Or, you can let your mind wander rather than concentrate on the words in the reading. Good readers follow along with the words, pausing briefly to recall background knowledge or similar experiences they have had in their lives. Let me show you how I activate my prior knowledge as we continue to read the next page (Block and Israel 2004, 158).*

**Grades 6–8** *What you know about a topic prior to reading about the topic is very important. After you begin reading, it is very important to think about your experiences and knowledge that are related to the information in the reading. You could just let your mind wander instead of concentrating on the words and details, but that wouldn't help you much. Good readers follow the author's words closely, and they pause to recall their background knowledge or similar experiences they've had in their lives. Let me show you the connections I make to what I already know as we continue to read the next page.*

# Think-Alouds and Comprehension-Monitoring Strategies for Mathematics *(cont.)*

## Activate Prior Knowledge Think-Aloud *(cont.)*

### Activity *(cont.)*

Using a transparency of a single page of mathematics text, point to specific sentences in which you connect relevant prior knowledge. Demonstrate how you activate your similar personal experiences and how you eliminate irrelevant or inaccurate prior knowledge. Read a sentence and describe an event from your personal experiences that contributes to the new information of that statement. Make the connections perfectly clear to students. Ask the class to practice and discuss activating prior knowledge. Have each student perform the think-aloud in small groups, then pairs, and finally in one-on-one conferences.

### Differentiation

It is very important that think-alouds be performed very slowly and that the words be enunciated very clearly for ELLs. Choose your words carefully and try to explain your thinking in a number of ways. Students reading below grade level should have the task modeled for them in their small groups by students who are reading at or above grade level. This will lower their anxiety levels for conducting their own think-alouds. While it may seem ideal to have gifted students model their thinking during reading for the rest of the class, do this with care. Some students may feel intimidated by the skills demonstrated. Be sure to focus on creating an atmosphere of mutual respect for think-alouds to incorporate gifted students' skills effectively.

# Think-Alouds and Comprehension-Monitoring Strategies for Mathematics *(cont.)*

## Determine Word Meanings Think-Aloud

### Background Information

Most students resort to skipping over words that they do not understand when they are reading. Looking up unknown words in the dictionary creates such an interruption for most readers that it causes them to disconnect from the reading. They lose their place and train of thought during the process and end up rereading a large selection of the text.

In nonfiction mathematics reading materials, it is common for writers to use long, difficult words that students have never encountered before. However, writers usually provide clues that help readers figure out the meanings of those words. It is important to teach students how to use the different types of context clues to decipher the meaning of unknown words. Using context clues effectively helps students develop better fluency and speed when reading, which encourages more pleasure reading and increases standardized test scores.

### Types of Context Clues

Many types of context clues are worthy of direct instruction to improve reading comprehension during mathematics instruction:

**Apposition or Definition Clues** Authors of nonfiction texts often provide synonyms or definitions of difficult words to help the reader understand the reading material. Usually, the definition or synonym is signaled to the reader by a comma, dash, parentheses, or words and phrases such as *or*, *is called*, *which means*, *who is*, *called*, *means*, *which is*, *that is*, and *in other words*.

*Example:* A variable, or a symbol for some value, is often represented by a letter such as "x."

**Example Clues** Writers provide examples that illustrate and clarify difficult to understand concepts or ideas. The example usually appears in the same sentence as the new word or in sentences that come before or after the word and can help students figure out the meaning of a new word or concept. The signal phrases for examples are *such as*, *including*, *for instance*, *to illustrate*, *are examples of*, *other examples*, and *for example*.

*Example:* A variable expression is an expression that contains a variable. For example, $(x + 7)$ is a variable expression.

**Contrast Clues** Writers sometimes indicate the meanings of difficult words or concepts through the presentation of the opposite meaning. Signals for opposition include *although*, *even though*, *yet*, *but*, *however*, *on the other hand*, and *in contrast*.

*Example:* A variable expression is an expression that contains a variable. However, a numerical expression contains only numbers.

## Determine Word Meanings Think-Aloud *(cont.)*

### Types of Context Clues *(cont.)*

**Modifier Clues** Sometimes modifiers (words that describe another word), such as adjectives, adverbs, or relative clauses, contain clues to a word's meaning. Relative clauses begin with *who*, *which*, *that*, *whose*, or *whom* and often explain or extend an idea or word in the main part of a sentence.

*Example:* A triangle is a shape that has 3 corners and 3 sides.

**Repetition Clues** Writers often repeat difficult words in familiar and new situations so that readers can figure out the meaning of the unknown words using their prior knowledge.

*Example:* A square is a shape with 4 corners and 4 sides. A square is also a type of parallelogram.

**Suggested Meaning Clues** When a sentence contains no specific clue words or explanations, the ideas in the sentence often suggest the meaning of words the students may not know. They should study the sentence as a whole and try to learn the meaning of the unknown word by asking questions about the information in the sentence. Students can draw on their prior knowledge and experience to help them decipher the meaning of the word.

*Example:* A pyramid contains 3 surface triangles and a square bottom.

### Grade Levels/Standards Addressed

Grades 1–2 (Standards 5.7, 7.4)
Grades 3–5 (Standards 5.5, 5.8)
Grades 6–8 (Standard 5.4)

### Activity

Prior to the reading of a selection from the textbook, ask students to locate any words they do not recognize or do not understand. Write the words on the board. Read the text aloud with the students. When you come to the word in question, say the following:

*This is a word I don't know. There are a few things I can do to help me figure out what this word means. First, I need to reread the sentence to see if I can figure it out. No, that didn't help. I'll try to read some sentences before and after the word to see if that might give me some clues. Are there any context clues? If not, maybe I can figure out the meaning by looking at the root word. Have I ever seen this word in another situation or book? What do I remember about it? I have read about this topic before. Let me think of things I remember about this topic to give me some clues.*

Be sure to let the students know that they do not have to go through all of the questions you model for them as you try to figure out the meaning of the word. They need to question themselves until they find a possible answer. Allow the students to use the clues to identify the meaning of the words they have selected. Encourage them to check the dictionary to determine if they were right. This will give them more confidence in using context clues.

# Think-Alouds and Comprehension–Monitoring Strategies for Mathematics *(cont.)*

## Determine Word Meanings Think-Aloud *(cont.)*

### Variation

Students in Grades 1–2 may not be able to read with great fluency, but they can still use context clues to decipher the meaning of unknown words. Teach them to use the following prompts for figuring out unknown words (Robb 2003):

- Did that sound right?
- Find the part that was not right.
- Take a good look at the beginning, middle, and end of the word.
- Does what you say match the letters you see?
- Can you think of another word it looks like?
- Can you say the word in chunks or syllables?
- Does the word have a prefix? What is it?
- Does the word have a suffix? What is it?
- Can you say what's left of the word?

### Differentiation

ELLs will benefit from one-on-one instruction with context clues during the explicit instruction phase. Students reading below grade level should be paired with strong readers during guided instruction and guided practice for modeling purposes and to provide extra support. It may be necessary to select an alternate section of the text for this activity for ELLs and students reading below grade level. Gifted students should be assigned to read a section of text appropriate for their reading level and encouraged to participate in the discussion of how to decipher unknown words so that their expert decoding skills can benefit the whole class when modeled.

# Think-Alouds and Comprehension–Monitoring Strategies for Mathematics *(cont.)*

## Predict Think-Aloud

### Background Information

Researchers have established that expert readers revise their understanding and predict as they read (Block and Pressley 2003). Making predictions in mathematics allows students to create a purpose for reading because they read to find out if their predictions are correct. It is effective for students to learn how to revise their predictions by watching and listening to their teachers model for them in the Predict Think-Aloud (based on Block and Israel 2004).

---

### Grade Levels/Standards Addressed

Grades 1–2 (Standard 5.7)
Grades 3–5 (Standards 5.8)
Grades 6–8 (Standard 5.4)

---

### Activity

Read a small section of text. Make some predictions about what might happen. To explain how to make accurate predictions, pause and describe what was in the text that helped you make your prediction. Keep reading, and deliver a Predict Think-Aloud. Say:

*My prediction is X. I have come to this prediction because the author left clues to tell me what would happen. The author used certain words and repeated phrases. Here are the questions that I asked myself while I was reading so that I could make predictions:*

- *What clues did the author give me?*
- *What did I already know that helped me to make a correct prediction?*
- *What did I miss that caused my prediction to be wrong? (Block and Israel 2004)*

Over the course of a few weeks, ask students to practice adding to, or changing, what they think to make predictions while they read.

### Differentiation

It is essential to model this think-aloud for ELLs because they may struggle to articulate how they came to their predictions. Slow the speech rate; choose appropriate words to describe the scene to the reader; and use an appropriate volume, intonation, and pauses to aid the students in understanding the meaning. Students reading below grade level should have a predictable text to work with as they learn how to monitor their own reading comprehension and determine the number of questions to ask for clarification of what they do not understand.

# Think-Alouds and Comprehension-Monitoring Strategies for Mathematics (cont.)

## Ask Questions Think-Aloud

### Background Information

Asking students questions about what they have read has long been a staple of education. Teachers traditionally check for students' successful comprehension through questioning. There is no doubt that students need to have the skills to answer questions successfully, but to do that, they should know how to generate and anticipate the questions worthy of asking. Reading researchers agree that expert readers ask and answer questions of themselves as they read to monitor their understanding of the material. Research shows that when students learn to generate questions about the text as they read, their overall comprehension improves (Yopp 1988 as cited by Duke and Pearson 2002). The Ask Questions Think-Aloud (Block and Israel 2004) is designed to assist students in checking the validity of their ideas, clarifying their thinking, or signaling that they need to reread or read ahead.

### Grade Levels/Standards Addressed

Grades 1–2 (Standard 5.7)
Grades 3–5 (Standards 5.5, 5.8)
Grades 6–8 (Standard 5.4)

### Activity

As students are reading a section of text independently, say:

**Grades 1–2** *Sometimes when I read, I don't understand. When I don't understand, I ask questions. I ask, 'What don't I understand? Is it a word I don't recognize? Can I break the word into chunks that I can recognize? Why doesn't the sentence make sense to me? Do I need to reread the sentence to see if I can figure it out, or should I read ahead to see if I can figure it out later? Can I look at the pictures to get a better idea of what it means?' After that, I ask myself questions like a journalist. 'Who or what is the main idea? What examples are being used? What words, illustrations, and examples help me understand the main idea?'*

**Grades 3–5** *Sometimes when I read, I get confused. When I don't understand something, I stop and ask myself questions. I ask, 'What don't I understand? Is it a word? Is it an example? Is it the way this sentence connects to the previous sentence? Is the sentence confusing? Is it a bigger idea than the one that occurred before? Is the sentence or example so long that I need to go back and reread, or should I go ahead and see if I can figure it out later?' After I ask myself questions like these, I can find the reason for my confusion and add whatever thoughts I need to read on with understanding. At that point, I can begin to ask myself questions so that I can summarize and remember what I have read. I ask myself, 'What is important? What is happening? Who or what is involved? Where is it happening? When is it happening? How does it happen? Why is it important? What examples are used? How do they help me understand important points?'*

# Think-Alouds and Comprehension-Monitoring Strategies for Mathematics *(cont.)*

## Ask Questions Think-Aloud *(cont.)*

### Activity *(cont.)*

**Grades 6–8** *Sometimes when I read, I come across sections that are confusing. Whenever I don't understand a word or a sentence, I remember that I need to stop and ask questions. I ask, 'What is it about this sentence or example that I don't understand? Is it a word? Is it the string of ideas connecting this sentence to the previous sentence? Is the sentence or example unclear? Is it a bigger idea than the one that has occurred before? Is the sentence or example so long that I need to go back and reread, or should I read ahead to get more context clues?' Once I have asked myself questions like these, I can find the reason for my confusion and add whatever thoughts I need to continue reading with understanding. I also need to ask myself questions so that I can summarize what I have read. I ask myself, 'What is important? What is happening? Who or what is involved? Where is it happening? How does it happen? Why is it important? What examples are used? How do they help me understand important points?'*

Read aloud more of the text to determine if the students' thinking is correct. Ask the students to use the same thought processes as they read the text silently from that point. Meet with the students individually and assess their abilities to ask questions by asking them to pause and describe their thinking as they read.

### Differentiation

ELLs may struggle to find the words to describe their thinking. It may help to have a list of words, phrases, or sentence frames available that are associated with think-alouds. Gifted students and students reading below grade level can use a reading selection that is appropriate for their reading levels; otherwise they may have too much or too little to consider when thinking about their struggles to understand the material.

# The Role of Questioning in Mathematics

## Questioning in Mathematics

Socrates said, "I have no answers, only questions." Thinking and learning are essentially extensions of questioning. Questioning is an integral part of the thinking process, and therefore, it is an essential element of learning. Students must develop their abilities to question in order to become successful problem-solvers, critical thinkers, and decision-makers. However, when young readers are asked questions by teachers, others, or themselves, they have difficulty answering them well (Report of the National Reading Panel 2000).

Perhaps the most prominent activities in a mathematics classroom are teacher questioning and answering the questions located in the textbook after the students have completed the reading. Obviously, question answering is an important feature of the classroom, but teachers should not limit its use for assessment purposes. While most of the questions to which students respond involve factual bits of information, these types of questions do not promote the development of learning about larger concepts. Questions that promote and emphasize the application of knowledge rather than the recall of facts help students develop reasoning abilities (Ryder and Graves 2003). Questions should be used to engage the students in the reading and help them apply their prior knowledge and cultural experiences to the reading.

## Questioning Should...

The teacher's goals in using questions to promote understanding include the following (Ryder and Graves 2003, p. 147):

- **Develop Interest and Motivate Students to Learn**—Provocative questions can generate student interest in the topic and get them more actively involved in their learning.

*Example:* If you were having a party for 20 people and needed to make 2 sandwiches per person, how many slices of bread would you need?

- **Highlight Lesson Content**—Questions can be used to point out important information, concepts, and ideas in the reading that are relevant to the learning objectives.

*Example:* What does it mean to distribute?

- **Integrate Lesson Content with What Students Have Studied and What They Already Know**—Questions should allow students to apply previously learned material to the content of a particular reading as well as apply their prior knowledge on the topic to the question.

*Example:* How does our understanding of money help us with decimals?

- **Structure High Level Understanding**—Questions should be sequenced in a way that encourages students to apply information to other situations or contexts. By focusing their attention on key concepts, then relating the concepts to a critical thinking question, students are given a scaffold to support higher-order thinking.

*Example:* Think about what it costs to buy a pair of shoes. If we pay $50 and the shoes are made and shipped from China, how much money do you think the worker in China receives from your $50? Is there only one worker, or are there several?

# The Role of Questioning in Mathematics *(cont.)*

## Questioning Should... *(cont.)*

- **Promote the Integration of Students' Knowledge, Values, and Cultural Background with Learning Objectives—** Learning becomes more relevant and meaningful when students are encouraged to draw on their knowledge and background. Students should be encouraged to construct meaning using their values, knowledge, and cultural perspective because in doing so they contribute to a richer and more stimulating environment.

  *Example:* Consider the shoes mentioned earlier. If they are $50, and made and shipped from China, how many companies or individuals are involved to get them to the local shoe store? Think of materials (leather, thread, rubber); packing (cardboard, paper); the ship; and its workers. Why do you suppose companies pay to have materials manufactured and shipped from overseas? What do you think are the pros and cons of making products in the United States instead?

## Types of Questions

While the purpose of questioning is to improve understanding, developing questions is an arduous task that requires the teacher to consider different cognitive levels of understanding information. Some questions can be answered easily because they are simple, factual questions. Other questions require great consideration and require the reader to integrate new information being learned with prior knowledge in order to formulate generalizations (Ryder and Graves 2003). While some educators classify questions into a few main categories (literal, interpretative, applied, open-ended), there are many other types of reading questions commonly asked of students on standardized tests. These types of questions ask students to understand or use main ideas, author's purpose, details, sequence, inference/prediction, literary techniques, fact/opinion, reading strategies, location of information/text organization, conventions, characterization, cause/effect, and vocabulary. Other researchers categorize questions within the framework of Bloom's Taxonomy. These levels, beginning with the most superficial and ending with the most complex, are knowledge, comprehension, application, analysis, synthesis, and evaluation.

## The Direct Instruction of Questioning

The goal of direct instruction of the question-answering strategy is to help teach readers how to become independent, active readers who can employ reading comprehension strategies to improve their understanding of the text. The Report of the National Reading Panel (2000) examined a number of studies on the effects of question-answering instruction and determined that students need question-answering instruction while reading so that they can learn and remember more from a text. The report found that direct instruction of the question-answering strategy leads to an improvement in answering questions after reading passages and in selecting strategies for finding answers in the text. Students should learn the steps to follow when answering questions and learn what to do when they cannot answer a question.

# The Role of Questioning in Mathematics *(cont.)*

## Steps to Answering Questions

Students follow a series of steps, either consciously or unconsciously, in order to respond to the questions asked of them. In the direct instruction of question-answering techniques, it is important to teach students the steps to follow. These steps include (Cotton 1988):

- Examining the question

- Deciphering the meaning of the question

- Looking back in the text to find the answer

- Formulating a response internally (thinking)

- Generating a response externally (saying, writing)

- Revising the response (based on the teacher's probing, discussion, and other feedback)

## What the Research Says

General investigations on the role of classroom questioning have revealed several important conclusions (Cotton 1988). Instruction that includes posing questions during reading is more effective in producing achievement gains than instruction without questioning students.

Furthermore, students perform better on test items previously asked as discussion questions than on items to which they have not been previously exposed. In addition, questions posed orally during classroom discussion are more effective in fostering learning than are written questions. Also, questions that highlight the important components of the reading result in better comprehension than questions that do not.

It is important to note that the placement and timing of questions have also proved to have an impact on student comprehension and achievement. Research shows that asking questions frequently during class discussion has a positive impact on students' ability to learn new information.

## Think Time and Wait Time

Researchers on questioning strategies also indicate that both *think time* and *wait time* impact student achievement. Think time is the amount of time the teacher allows to elapse after he or she has posed a question and before the student begins to speak. Wait time refers to the amount of time a teacher waits after a student has stopped speaking before saying anything.

## Think Time and Wait Time *(cont.)*

Increasing both think and wait times during oral questioning results in (Cotton 1988):

- improving student achievement and retention of information

- increasing the number of higher-level thinking responses in students

- increasing the length of student responses

- increasing the number of unsolicited responses

- decreasing students' failure to respond to questions

- increasing the amount and quality of evidence students offer to support their inferences

- increasing the contributions made by students who do not participate much when wait time is shorter

- expanding the variety of responses offered by students

- decreasing student interruptions

- increasing student-to-student interactions

- increasing the number of questions posed by students

## Self-Questioning

While students should be expected to successfully answer questions posed by their teachers and their textbook about the reading, researchers have found that engaging students in the process of generating questions about the text as they read improves their ability to comprehend (Duke and Pearson 2002). Students should be actively engaged in asking questions during mathematics reading, and the classroom should be such that students are encouraged to ask questions. Without training, young readers are not likely to question themselves or use questions spontaneously to make inferences. Research shows that when readers are taught how to generate questions, they better engage in the text by asking questions that lead to the development of better memory representations. The goal is to teach students to self-question while reading. If readers ask *why*, *how*, *when*, *where*, *what*, and *who* questions, it is possible for them to integrate sections of the text, which thereby improves comprehension in mathematics and memory for what is read, and enables them to gain a deeper understanding of the text. Question generation is a metacognitive skill that increases the students' awareness of whether or not they understand what they are reading.

The Report of the National Reading Panel (2000) cites Rosenshine, Meister, and Chapman's (1996) meta-analysis of 30 studies that instructed students how to generate questions during reading. These studies demonstrated that there is strong empirical and scientific evidence that reading comprehension is benefited by instruction of question generation during reading in terms of memory and answering questions based on text as well as integrating and identifying main ideas through summarization.

# Questioning Strategies for Mathematics

## Previewing the Text Through Questioning

### Background Information

One way to stimulate students to ask questions is to have them preview the mathematics text by looking at the pictures included in the reading. Previewing the Text Through Questioning is an effective pre-reading activity that enables students to develop questioning skills (Hoyt 2002). Before the class reads the text together, the teacher guides the students as they look at each picture included in the reading selection. The teacher marks an important image in the text with a sticky note and asks the students to begin on that page rather than at the beginning of the selection. As the students focus on developing questions about the pictures, they activate their prior knowledge on the topic. They use prediction skills to hazard answers to their own questions, and they are encouraged to reflect on the accuracy of their question-answering skills after reading in order to help them develop stronger metacognitive skills.

### Grade Levels/Standards Addressed
Grades 1–2 (Standard 5.2)
Grades 3–5 (Standard 5.3)

### Activity

Determine the reading selection to be introduced to the students. Invite students to preview the reading by looking at all of the pictures and examples as a class. Model the strategy by thinking aloud as you examine the examples and encourage students to share their thoughts. Ask students to choose the example that they believe is most important and have them explain their choice. Have students develop questions about the example and the reading selection, and write these on sticky notes.

Point out moments during the question generating when students are relying on their prior knowledge. Encourage them to predict the answers to their questions. Summarize the questions and the students' answers for the class and then ask students to read the selection. Have students reflect on their pre-reading questions and answers by asking them to identify which questions they answered correctly during the preview, why they were able to answer the questions, and which questions they discovered answers to.

Students can preview the reading in small groups and then independently by using the Previewing the Text Through Questioning (Hoyt 2002) handout (page 130). Stop the students before they complete the reading to share and discuss their questions and the possible answers. Ask them to justify and explain their predictions.

### Differentiation

ELLs may need to have the text read aloud to them as they complete the activity independently or in small groups. It may help to allow students reading below grade level to complete the handout orally, and have a classmate write down the students' answers. Encourage gifted students to develop higher-level questions before they read so that they can look into causes, experiences, and facts to draw a conclusion or make connections to other areas of learning.

# Questioning Strategies for Mathematics *(cont.)*

## Previewing the Text Through Questioning *(cont.)*

### Grades 1–2 Example

| Previewing Questions | |
|---|---|
| **As I previewed the images, my questions were:** | **Possible answers:** |
| How do the numbers on the clock mean minutes? | They must somehow go up to 45 because I have heard people say things like "2:45 P.M." |
| How do you tell what the hour is if the little hand is between two numbers? | Whichever number comes up next is probably the hour. |

| After-Reading Reflections |
|---|
| **What were the questions I answered correctly during the preview about?** |
| How the numbers mean minutes and that the long hand on the 6 means thirty minutes. |
| **Why was I able to answer the questions correctly?** |
| I remember learning something about the clock last year. |
| **What questions can I now answer after reading?** |
| How do you tell what the hour is if the little hand is between the two numbers?  How do the numbers on the clock mean minutes?  What time is it? |

### Grades 3–5 Example

| Previewing Questions | |
|---|---|
| **As I previewed the images, my questions were:** | **Possible answers:** |
| How do you know whether to use feet or inches to measure the perimeter? | If the object is big, you would use feet.  If the object is small, you would use inches. |
| What are some reasons you would need to know how to find the perimeter of something? | Maybe if you were going to run or drive around something, you would want to know the distance. |

| After-Reading Reflections |
|---|
| **What were the questions I answered correctly during the preview about?** |
| How you choose to use feet or inches and why you might measure perimeter. |
| **Why was I able to answer the questions correctly?** |
| I remember running around the track in P.E. |
| **What questions can I now answer after reading?** |
| What shapes have sides that are the same length, so you can use multiplication instead of just addition?  How do you measure the perimeter of a circle since it has no straight sides? |

**Name:** _____

# Previewing the Text Through Questioning

**Directions:** Before you begin reading, preview the text and write down your questions and possible answers. After reading, write your answers to the reflection questions.

| Previewing Questions | |
|---|---|
| **As I previewed the images, my questions were:** | **Possible answers:** |
| _____ | _____ |
| _____ | _____ |
| _____ | _____ |
| _____ | _____ |

| After-Reading Reflections |
|---|
| **What were the questions I answered correctly during the preview about?** |
| _____ |
| _____ |
| _____ |
| **Why was I able to answer the questions correctly?** |
| _____ |
| _____ |
| _____ |
| **What questions can I now answer after reading?** |
| _____ |
| _____ |
| _____ |
| _____ |

Adapted from Linda Hoyt, *Make It Real*, [Portsmouth, NH: Heinemann, 2002], 125.

## Scaffolding Reader Questions

### Background Information

It is essential to encourage students to verbalize and record their questions when developing questioning skills in order to improve reading comprehension. This helps readers anticipate questions in the future and develops their reasoning skills. When students are young, teachers can help readers formulate and record their questions, but as they become more fluent readers, they can record their own questions. The Scaffolding Reader Questions strategy (Hoyt 2002) enables the students to develop questions before, during, and after reading. The teacher should model how to construct questions during each of the reading phases for the students to make the process clear.

### Grade Levels/Standards Addressed

Grades 1–2 (Standard 8.2)
Grades 3–5 (Standard 8.2)
Grades 6–8 (Standard 8.2)

### Activity

Distribute copies of the Scaffolding Reader Questions handout (page 134). Before students begin reading a particular selection, ask them to conduct a preview in which they look at the title, table of contents, headings, key vocabulary, pictures, diagrams, and other elements. Have students create questions based on the preview.

They must be specific about how the preview leads them to the questions. Have students share their questions with the entire class and explain how the preview led them to the questions. Next, instruct students to begin reading the selection. During guided reading, pause and ask them to record important items worthy of noting. Before students continue reading, they must record questions that will allow them to further their understanding and learning on the topic. Finally, ask students to record questions that the reading did not address but that they want to find the answers to.

### Differentiation

ELLs will benefit from having the process modeled for them. They may need a list of words to help them complete the activity. Provide extra time for students reading below grade level to produce questions. Be sure to write down the questions students generate based on their previews on an overhead or the board for the class to review and use as a guide. Gifted students should be encouraged to ask higher-level thinking questions to make connections to other topics and areas of learning.

# Questioning Strategies for Mathematics *(cont.)*

## Scaffolding Reader Questions *(cont.)*

### Grades 1–2 Example

| Before-Reading Questions | |
|---|---|
| **Based on my preview of...** | **My questions are:** |
| title | What is an array? |
| examples | Why are all the numbers lined up like that? |

| During-Reading Questions | |
|---|---|
| **While I was reading, I noticed...** | **My questions are:** |
| An array is "numbers displayed in rows and columns." | How do I figure out how many rows and columns? |
| It helps me understand multiplication. | How is addition like multiplication? |

| After-Reading Questions | |
|---|---|
| **I still wonder about...** | **My questions are:** |
| the link between addition and multiplication | Is there a faster way to find the answer without making an array? |

### Grades 3–5 Example

| Before-Reading Questions | |
|---|---|
| **Based on my preview of...** | **My questions are:** |
| title | What are the different kinds of angles? |
| bold words | What is an acute or obtuse angle? |

| During-Reading Questions | |
|---|---|
| **While I was reading, I noticed...** | **My questions are:** |
| The book talks about three different kinds of angles. | What angle is it when you cut a pizza in half? |
| Acute means less than 90 degrees and obtuse means more than 90 degrees. | Are acute and obtuse angles related to each other? |

| After-Reading Questions | |
|---|---|
| **I still wonder about...** | **My questions are:** |
| the relationship between angles and cutting into something | Does the acute, obtuse, and right angle rule work if you cut into a square cake instead of a round pizza? |
| the angles of other fractions | What angle is linked to one-fifth or one-eighth? |

Adapted from Linda Hoyt, *Make It Real*, [Portsmouth, NH: Heinemann, 2002], 125.

## Scaffolding Reader Questions *(cont.)*

### Grades 6–8 Example

| Before-Reading Questions | |
|---|---|
| **Based on my preview of…** | **My questions are:** |
| title | What is a linear function? |
| bold words | What is a slope? |
| examples | How does a linear function relate to a person climbing a mountain? |

| During-Reading Questions | |
|---|---|
| **While I was reading, I noticed…** | **My questions are:** |
| A linear function involves both an $x$ variable and a $y$ variable. | If the big idea of algebra is to find the value of the variable, what do we do when we have both $x$ and $y$? |
| Slope seems to be related to the steepness of the line. | If the slope is a high number, does that mean the line is more steep or less steep? |
| Linear functions are linked to many real world experiences, like skiing downhill. | Are there experiences that you can use linear functions for that do not involve hills and mountains? |

| After-Reading Questions | |
|---|---|
| **I still wonder about…** | **My questions are:** |
| finding the slope | What happens if the slope is negative? |
| putting an equation in the right format | How do you find the intercepts and slopes if the equation is in the wrong format? (i.e., $8x + 2y = 12$, instead of $y = -4x + 6$) |

Adapted from Linda Hoyt, *Make It Real*, [Portsmouth, NH: Heinemann, 2002], 125.

**Name:** _____

# Scaffolding Reader Questions

**Directions:** Before you read, preview the text and write down your questions. While you read, take notes of what you notice in the text and write down your questions. After reading, write down what questions you still have about the topic.

| Before-Reading Questions | |
|---|---|
| **Based on my preview of...** | **My questions are:** |
| _____ | _____ |
| _____ | _____ |
| _____ | _____ |
| _____ | _____ |

| During-Reading Questions | |
|---|---|
| **While I was reading, I noticed...** | **My questions are:** |
| _____ | _____ |
| _____ | _____ |
| _____ | _____ |
| _____ | _____ |

| After-Reading Questions | |
|---|---|
| **I still wonder about...** | **My questions are:** |
| _____ | _____ |
| _____ | _____ |
| _____ | _____ |
| _____ | _____ |

Adapted from Linda Hoyt, *Make It Real*, [Portsmouth, NH: Heinemann, 2002], 125.

# Coding the Text

## Background Information

It is essential for students to self-monitor as they read so that they can check their understanding and use fix-up strategies if needed. Coding the Text is an activity that helps students generate questions about the text and develop their metacognitive skills. This activity teaches students how to deal with areas of confusion when reading. The teacher performs a think-aloud when introducing the activity so that the students have a model for completing the task. During Coding the Text, students use sticky notes to mark the moments in the reading that are confusing and things they want to know more about.

### Grade Levels/Standards Addressed

Grades 1–2 (Standard 8.2)
Grades 3–5 (Standard 8.2)
Grades 6–8 (Standard 8.2)

## Activity

Write the codes on the board that students should use to make notes about the reading.

| ? | *I am confused/I don't understand* |
| M | *I want to learn more about this* |
| * | *This is important* |
| N | *New information* |
| C | *Connection* |
| TH | *Theme of the text* |
| AHA | *Big idea in the text* |

Emergent readers should be limited to the first two codes while more fluent readers can use more codes. Distribute sticky notes to the students and instruct them to place the notes in the text and code the text as they read. After students code the text, instruct them to generate questions based on the codes they have created. Share the questions in a classroom discussion in which the students attempt to answer the questions and generate more.

## Differentiation

ELLs may benefit from hearing the reading selection read aloud as they follow along. Students reading below grade level should use only three codes as they read, as too many might overwhelm them. Gifted students should be encouraged to explain why they placed the codes in the locations they did; push them to generate higher-order thinking questions.

# Questioning Strategies for Mathematics *(cont.)*

## Burning Questions

### Background Information

The Burning Questions activity is similar to Coding the Text, but it is a whole-group rather than an individual or small-group activity. In order to enhance the students' self-monitoring abilities and metacognitive skills about reading, the teacher instructs students to formulate questions for a large classroom discussion. During the discussion, students present the questions and the teacher can address and clarify any moments in the reading that cause confusion for the readers.

### Grade Levels/Standards Addressed

Grades 3–5 (Standard 8.2)
Grades 6–8 (Standard 8.2)

### Activity

Assign a reading selection for the students to complete independently. Distribute a number of sticky notes to each student, depending on the length of the reading selection. Instruct the students to use the sticky notes to mark where they experience confusion and to generate questions about the information in the reading.

After collecting the sticky notes, present the questions anonymously to the entire class. With each question, clarify the points of confusion by going back through the text, looking at headings, finding the main ideas, examining key words and examples, etc.

### Differentiation

ELLs may be confused by the entire reading assignment, so it may be helpful to have the selection read aloud to them. Provide a variety of visual supports and explain concepts in multiple ways. Students reading below grade level will appreciate the anonymity of the activity; pay close attention to their questions during the whole-class discussion and think aloud to demonstrate how to use fix-up strategies. Encourage gifted students to generate questions about the reading according to the framework of Bloom's Taxonomy. The levels of this framework, beginning with the most superficial and ending with the most complex, are knowledge, comprehension, application, analysis, synthesis, and evaluation.

# ReQuest

## Background Information

The ReQuest activity (Manzo 1969, as cited by Lenski, Wham, and Johns 1999) boosts students' reading comprehension by modeling how to ask their own questions about their reading. When students ask questions of themselves while reading, they learn how to monitor their own understanding of the text, and they have better comprehension as a result. The ReQuest activity can be used with individuals, small groups, or the whole class. It is an interactive questioning technique that increases students' motivation to read.

### Grade Levels/Standards Addressed

Grades 3–5 (Standard 8.2)
Grades 6–8 (Standard 8.2)

## Activity

Choose a reading selection for the students that contains many new ideas that may be challenging to them. First introduce the ReQuest activity by modeling its use. Use examples from a reading selection previously read by the students. Begin by reading the first paragraph of the text aloud. Then ask and answer questions about the contents of the passage. Model for the students how you formulate your answers and try to give examples, if possible, in your answers.

For example, the reading selection may discuss the area and surface area of objects. Model question-asking for students: *What is the difference between area and surface area? How do I figure out the area of a shape? How do I figure out surface area? If I continue reading, I see that area has to do with two-dimensional shapes, like a square, while surface area has to do with three-dimensional shapes, like a cube. So, if I were to calculate the area of a square, I would just multiply the base value by the height. But for a cube, I would have to multiply my answer for a square by 6, since a cube has 6 sides.*

Ask the students to read the next section of the text. Limit this section to no more than a paragraph or two in length. Instruct the students to take turns in asking you questions about what they read, and answer the questions as you modeled for them previously. Ask the students to continue reading the next section of the text, and inform them that you will be asking them questions about the section and they will be answering your questions. Continue to alternate between student-generated questions and teacher-generated questions until the entire passage is read. Remind the students to ask questions of themselves as they read because, in doing so, they can monitor their understanding and improve their comprehension.

## Differentiation

Preteach the reading assignment to ELLs in advance so that class time is review. Provide ample think- and wait-time throughout the activity. It is usually helpful to give ELLs a vocabulary list to assist them with the reading material. Write the questions asked and the answers provided on the board or on an overhead projector for students reading below grade level to study. Type up the questions and answers and distribute them to use as a study guide. Gifted students should be encouraged to ask challenging questions that go beyond the material in the reading. They can find the answers through independent research.

# Questioning Strategies for Mathematics *(cont.)*

## Question Journal

### Background Information

An informal but effective and useful way to help students learn questioning skills is through a Question Journal. Teachers distribute small journals for students to record their questions about what they read over the course of the term. Students use their journals to ask questions and answer questions that are asked of them. The teacher directs students to generate the questions before, during, and after reading. By providing students with a specific location for the exclusive recording of questions and their answers, the teacher focuses on teaching students how to anticipate questions about the reading. Furthermore, the teacher instructs students to link the questions to Bloom's Taxonomy in their efforts to encourage higher-order questioning and thinking skills.

### Grade Levels/Standards Addressed

Grades 3–5 (Standard 8.2)
Grades 6–8 (Standard 8.2)

### Activity

Distribute small, paperbound journals to the students and explain to them that the Question Journals (page 140) will be used for reading assignments throughout the term. Instruct students to record the title of the reading selection and the date, and then record questions they have about the reading. Instruct students to leave adequate room to answer their own questions and any other questions that may arise from the reading. Show an example of a completed entry on a transparency so that students can see the correct format for a question journal. Have students share their questions during a whole-class discussion. Use the discussion to solicit possible answers from students and discuss other ways to ask the same question. Be sure to have students link the questions to Bloom's Taxonomy, and use the discussion to modify the questions for higher levels of the framework. These levels, beginning with the most superficial and ending with the most complex, are knowledge, comprehension, application, analysis, synthesis, and evaluation.

### Differentiation

Write down the questions and answers on the board or on an overhead transparency for ELLs and students reading below grade level. Be sure to rephrase and repeat important words and concepts during the discussion and allow adequate think and wait time after posing questions to the class. Gifted students should be encouraged to explore the concepts of interest to them in the reading in greater depth through independent research. They should also be encouraged to explore higher levels of questioning in Bloom's framework.

# Questioning Strategies for Mathematics (cont.)

## Question Journal (cont.)

### Grades 3–5 Example

Reading Selection: <u>"Mean, Median & Mode"</u>                    Date: <u>January 16</u>

| Before-Reading Questions | Possible Answers |
|---|---|
| What is *mean*? (Knowledge) <br> What is *median*? (Knowledge) <br> What is *mode*? (Knowledge) | I think *mean* is the sum of a list of numbers. <br> I think *median* is the number that is in the middle. <br> I think *mode* is the highest number in the list. |
| **During-Reading Questions** | **Possible Answers** |
| Is *mean* the same as *average*? (Comprehension) <br> When would someone ever need to know the mode of a list? (Application) | I think that *mean* and *average* mean the same thing. <br> If you wanted to know the most popular topping for a pizza, the mode could be useful. |
| **After-Reading Questions** | **Possible Answers** |
| Is there a time when you should use the word *mean* and a time when you should only use the word *average*? (Analysis) <br> Is the median the number that is mathematically in the middle, or is it the number that is physically in the middle of the list? (Comprehension) | I know that in baseball, they use the word *average* and never say *mean*, so I guess it depends on the situation. <br> I think the median is physically the middle number. |

### Grades 6–8 Example

Reading Selection: <u>"Systems of Equations"</u>                    Date: <u>January 16</u>

| Before-Reading Questions | Possible Answers |
|---|---|
| What are *systems of equations*? (Knowledge) <br> Do you have to graph them in order to solve them? (Knowledge) | Maybe there are two equations that each have an $x$ and a $y$ variable. <br> It is possible to use graphing to find the answers. |
| **During-Reading Questions** | **Possible Answers** |
| When you graph two equations together, is the intersection of the graphs the answer to the system? (Comprehension) | I think that the intersection is the answer to the system. |
| **After-Reading Questions** | **Possible Answers** |
| What is the answer if the graphs of the lines never intersect? (Knowledge) <br> What is the answer if the graphs of the lines overlap? (Knowledge) <br> Are there ways of solving systems of equations that do not involve graphing? (Synthesis) | Perhaps the equations would have no real solution. <br><br> Overlapping lines have every number in common, so I think the answer would be all the numbers. <br> If you made one equation equal the $x$ value, you could plug that in for $x$ in the second equation. |

**Name:** _____

# Question Journal

Reading Selection: _____ Date: _____

| Before-Reading Questions | Possible Answers |
|---|---|
|  |  |

| During-Reading Questions | Possible Answers |
|---|---|
|  |  |

| After-Reading Questions | Possible Answers |
|---|---|
|  |  |

## Beat the Teacher

### Background Information

Beat the Teacher (Hoyt 2002) is another questioning activity that helps students develop strong questioning skills that can enhance their reading comprehension. As students read the text, they generate questions that they pose to the teacher. The activity motivates students to try to stump their teacher with their questions. Their goal is to ask a question the teacher cannot answer about the assigned reading. The activity increases student motivation to read and reread in their quest to stump the teacher, and in the process of generating challenging questions and posing them to their teacher, they must listen to and pay attention to the teacher's answers. To challenge the students further and create a competition, the activity can be modified to engage the students in question answering. Every time the teacher answers a question correctly, the students must answer a teacher question, and points are tallied on the board for correct answers.

### Grade Levels/Standards Addressed

Grades 3–5 (Standard 8.2)
Grades 6–8 (Standard 8.2)

### Activity

Assign a reading selection to the students to complete in small groups or paired reading. Instruct the students to read the selection with great care. Explain that the goal is to generate very challenging questions that the teacher cannot answer about the reading. Read the selection silently as the students are reading and writing questions, and stop often to write your own questions about the text. When the time for reading and question generation is complete, take a seat in the front of the room, and have the students ask their questions about the text in an orderly fashion. Ask one student to record the questions and answers so that you can give them to the students to review later.

### Differentiation

Provide ELLs with plenty of time to generate questions. It may help to give them the reading assignment the day before so that they can have adequate time to process the information. Have students write down the questions they pose and the answers you give on the board or on an overhead transparency so that students reading below grade level can see them. Model how you examine a question and formulate your answer through detailed think-alouds. Gifted students should be encouraged to find the answers to any questions posed that you cannot answer.

# Questioning Strategies for Mathematics *(cont.)*

## Questioning the Author

### Background Information

Questioning the Author (QtA) (Beck, McKeown, Hamilton, and Kucan 1997) is an activity that helps students understand, analyze, and elaborate on an author's meaning and intent as they read a text. The purpose of QtA is to engage readers beyond the factual, surface-level information to help them understand the ideas and concepts represented in the text. This strategy also helps students understand that a text represents an author's ideas and attitude and helps them to understand what the author is attempting to communicate. Teachers probe students' understanding through a series of questions called *queries*. Queries encourage students to work together during student-to-student interactions to construct meaning as they read and reflect on the text. Queries help students engage in working with the ideas in a text. They are used when students are engaged in reading a short passage (such as a one-page lesson) rather than at the conclusion of a longer reading. Most teachers use conventional questioning associated with reading (*Who? What? Why?*), but queries are purposefully open-ended to encourage multiple answers and divergent thinking (Clark and Graves 2005).

To help students along, ask the following types of questions during QtA (Clark and Graves 2005; Ryder and Graves 2003; Beck, et al. 1997; Lenski, Wham, and Johns 1999):

**Initiating Queries** (for identifying ideas in the text):

- What is the author's purpose?
- What is the author talking about?

**Follow-Up Queries** (for connecting ideas in the text to construct meaning):

- Why did the author include this illustration/photograph/numbered list?
- Why do you think the author says that right here?
- How does that connect with what the author has already told us on this page?
- Does that make sense with what the author told us in a previous lesson/unit?
- Did the author explain it clearly?
- Does the author explain why?
- How did the author show us the differences between these two concepts?
- Is there anything missing?
- What do we need to find out?

### Grade Levels/Standards Addressed

Grades 3–5 (Standard 8.2)
Grades 6–8 (Standard 8.2)

## Questioning the Author *(cont.)*

### Preparation

Read through the text selection very carefully to identify the most important concepts and ideas. Develop the questions to present to the students based on important themes you find compelling. Break up the reading selection into smaller segments that will be read and then discussed by the students. Develop the queries that focus on essential ideas and concepts in the reading and on each of the text segments to be presented.

### Activity

Inform the students that they will be taking a different approach to reading in the activity. Tell them that they will be reading a series of short segments of text. Once they have finished reading one segment, they will hold a class discussion about its meaning. Explain to the students that a person wrote the text, and that in order to understand the author's intentions or purpose, it helps to discuss the text and the possibilities in detail. Direct the students to read the first segment of the text. When they are finished, ask the class to initiate queries on the list in relationship to the reading. Encourage students to answer and respond to one another's questions and comments and to use the text to support their positions. Direct students to read the next segment of the text and ask them the follow-up queries in relationship to the reading. Have the students discuss the meaning of the passage with the class.

### Differentiation

ELLs will need the reading broken up into small enough sections so that they can effectively focus their attention. Each passage should involve a limited number of ideas and concepts to reduce the chances that the students reading below grade level will have trouble understanding the text. Gifted students may prefer to work independently or in a small homogenous group.

# Summarizing in Mathematics

## The Challenge of Summarizing

Reading research indicates that summarizing is a skill that is difficult for students to learn, but it offers tremendous benefits to readers (Duke and Pearson 2002). Summarizing improves readers' abilities to locate the main ideas and supporting details, identify and omit unnecessary details and redundant material, remember what is read, analyze text structure, see how ideas are related, generalize details, clarify meaning, take notes, and rethink what they have read so that they can process it more deeply.

When students summarize their reading, they distill large sections of text, extract the most essential information, and then create a coherent, more concise text that relates the same information as the original text. In order to effectively summarize, readers must be able to identify the main idea and differentiate important information from unimportant information; this serves to stress the most vital parts and minimize less relevant details.

When expert readers tackle a text, they stop periodically to summarize what they have read as a way to monitor their own comprehension and processing of the text. They mentally "put together" or reconstruct what they have read so far so that they can continue to process the text when they continue reading.

When summarizing, students pay much closer attention to what is read. They spend more time on reading and trying to understand what they are reading. This enables them to integrate ideas and generalize from the text information.

Condensing text so that the substance of a reading selection is in brief form is no easy task and often leads to artificial, awkward language and organization. Reading experts suggest that reading comprehension is further improved by revising summaries so that they sound more natural when read because students will remember the information better. Students remember revised summaries better because they are written in the students' own words. Reading research indicates that students are more successful at synthesizing information if they put the information in their own words. When students translate the ideas they have read into their own words, they can more easily retrieve that information to accomplish a learning task. Students must use their own words to form connections across the concepts and relate the concepts to their own prior knowledge and experiences.

## The Steps in Summarizing

Students need to remember three important elements to summarize effectively. Students must keep the information in their summaries brief, identify the most important ideas, and mention some supporting details (adapted from Hoyt 2002).

# Summarizing in Mathematics *(cont.)*

## The Steps in Summarizing *(cont.)*

A synthesis of the steps provided by reading researchers (Duke and Pearson 2002) are as follows:

- Delete unnecessary material.
- Delete redundant material.
- Provide a name for categories or list of details.
- Identify and use the author's main ideas.
- Select or construct a topic sentence.

Instructing students to follow these steps when summarizing gives them a framework, exercises their metacognitive skills, and improves their overall ability to comprehend reading materials.

## The Main Idea

One of the skills involved in summarizing and retelling is locating the main idea. In order to summarize, students must be able to identify the key concepts or chief topic of a passage, a paragraph, and a sentence. The main idea is the central thought, and because it seems so obvious to skilled readers, it can be overlooked as an important element when teaching students how to summarize. At times, the main topic of the passage is not directly stated but rather is implied indirectly. Therefore, students need instruction and practice in locating the main idea, as it is the one idea to which all other sentences in a passage relate.

## Quick and Easy Main Idea Activities

The following activities are fast, easy ways to highlight how to locate the main idea in reading passages (Dechant 1991):

- Have students categorize objects or words from a passage. This helps them comprehend the main ideas.

  *Example: Let's classify the different linear functions as sloping upward or downward.*

- Instruct students to identify the main idea of specific sentences by underlining key words.

  *Example: Let's highlight the rules for figuring out the direction of a linear function.*

- Ask students to locate the topic sentence or the key sentence that best identifies the main idea of a paragraph.

  *Example: Which sentence best tells the main idea about linear functions?*

- Have students write a title for a paragraph or a passage. Have the students read a newspaper story on a mathematics topic and remove the title. Ask the students to give the story an appropriate title and then compare it to the actual title used in the paper.

# Summarizing in Mathematics *(cont.)*

## Summarizing vs. Retelling

Is retelling the same as summarizing? Teachers of emergent readers frequently ask students to retell what they have just read, but retelling is different than summarizing. Summarizing forces the reader to condense the information by omitting trivial information. Summarizing involves developing skills in deletion, inference, and making generalizations. Retelling does not involve reducing the text into a more brief statement. When students retell what they have read, they paraphrase information. To teach students how to summarize effectively, they should first build their retelling skills and then move on to condensing information while summarizing.

## What the Research Says

The Report of the National Reading Panel (2000) analyzed 18 different studies on the direct instruction of summarizing in reading and reveals that summarization improves readers' comprehension of text (Trabasso and Bouchard 2002). When students are taught how to create summaries, their ability to summarize improves and the quality of their summaries improves. Readers improve the quality of their summaries by identifying main ideas, omitting details, including ideas related to the main idea, generalizing, and removing redundancy. Teachers should train students to summarize automatically as they read so that they are consistently monitoring their comprehension of the text.

# Summarizing Strategies for Mathematics

## Read, Cover, Remember, Retell

### Background Information

The Read, Cover, Remember, Retell (RCRR) activity (Hoyt 2002) is an effective approach to help readers at all grade levels who think that good reading is reading quickly and as a result do not understand what they have read. The technique is modeled for students during a whole-class instruction period, and then conducted with students who work as partners to read the same text. Students silently read a small portion of the text—about the size that they could cover with their hand. After reading, they cover the text, turn to their partner, and try to remember and retell what they just read. If they leave out any information, their partner can fill in the missing details. They then switch roles to read the next section. Because mathematics reading is predominantly informational text, this approach is particularly effective for training students to develop their summarization skills. Students can gradually use the strategy as they read independently.

### Grade Levels/Standards Addressed

Grades 1–2 (Standard 7.3)
Grades 3–5 (Standard 7.5)
Grades 6–8 (Standard 7.3)

### Activity

Model the Read, Cover, Remember, Retell strategy by using the think-aloud technique. Pair students and assign a selection of text for them to read. Instruct both students to begin reading a small portion of the text silently, using the size of the hand to determine how much information to read.

After reading, one student covers the text, turns to the partner, and tries to retell it using his or her own words. The partner should then evaluate the quality of the retelling and fill in any missing information. Students switch roles for the next section of reading. When the partners have completed the reading, they can write a summary of the entire reading selection and share them with the class. Use an overhead projector to evaluate and elaborate on how the summaries can be more effective, etc.

### Differentiation

It might help ELLs to have their partners read the section of text aloud to them rather than ask them to read it silently. Students reading below grade level and gifted students should have a text that is appropriate for their levels.

### Read, Cover, Remember, Retell

- Read only as much as your hand can cover.
- Cover the words with your hand.
- Remember what you have just read (it is okay to take another look).
- Retell what you have just read in your own words.

# Summarizing Strategies for Mathematics (cont.)

## Read, Cover, Remember, Retell (cont.)

### Grades 1–2 Example

**Original Text:**
Jim has 3 red balls. Jill has 6 yellow balls. If they put them together, how many balls will they have total?

**Student Retell:**
We need to find out how many balls there are altogether. There are 3 red balls. There are 6 yellow balls.

### Grades 3–5 Example

**Original Text:**
Jane and Frank are planning a party for their class. They are going to provide 2 hot dogs with buns, a scoop of potato salad, and a cup of juice for each person in the class. If there are 36 people in the class, how many hot dogs, buns, and cups do they need to buy for the party?

**Student Retell:**
We need to find out how many hot dogs, buns, and cups Jane and Frank need to buy for their party. They have 36 people in their class. They want everyone to have 2 hot dogs with buns. They want everyone to have 1 cup of juice. They are also going to give everyone 1 scoop of potato salad.

### Grades 6–8 Example

**Original Text:**
Mrs. Nelson is going to buy textbooks for each of her 6 math classes. Her first class is Algebra I, and the books are $69.99 each plus a one-time-only fixed charge of $25 to reinforce the binding of all Algebra I books. Her second class is Pre-Algebra and the textbooks are $47.99 each plus one-time-only fixed charge of $15 to reinforce the binding of all the Pre-Algebra books. Her third class is Physical Science and the books are $89.95 each plus a one-time-only fixed charge of $30 to reinforce the binding of all Physical Science books. Create a linear equation for each book order and graph them on a single coordinate plane. How many of each kind of book could she buy if she were given $1,500 per class?

**Student Retell:**
We need to find out how many Algebra I books we can buy for $1,500, how many Pre-Algebra books we could buy for $1,500, and how many Physical Science books we could buy for $1,500. We know that Algebra books cost $69.99 with a $25 additional fee. Pre-Algebra books are $47.99 plus a $15 additional fee. Physical Science books are $89.95 plus a $30 additional fee. We also need to show our equations and graph them on one coordinate plane.

# Summarizing Strategies for Mathematics *(cont.)*

## Rank-Ordering Retell

### Background Information

Students need to learn how to evaluate the information in a mathematics selection to determine the most important ideas, moderately important ideas, and the least important ideas to effectively summarize what they have read. Rank-Ordering Retell (Hoyt 2002) assists students in learning to identify the main idea and supporting details. In the activity, students write down phrases they consider to be important to the topic taken from the reading either directly or indirectly. These phrases should describe the content of the reading. The students must decide if the phrases can be categorized as the most important, moderately important, or least important. In small groups or as a whole class, students learn how to rank the importance of the information as they justify their placement of the phrases into the different categories.

### Grade Levels/Standards Addressed
Grades 1–2 (Standard 7.3)
Grades 3–5 (Standard 7.5)
Grades 6–8 (Standard 7.3)

### Activity

Distribute strips of paper. As students begin a reading selection, ask them to write down phrases they consider important to the topic. The phrases can be either taken directly from the reading or inferred by the students and should describe the information in the reading. Ask students to use the Rank-Ordering Retell handout (page 151) to begin evaluating and sorting the strips into three categories: most important, moderately important, and least important. Instruct them to work with the most important and least important first, as this is the easiest way to evaluate the information. Have students justify their decision to place the phrases in the different categories. Ask students to identify which ideas would be the most helpful if they had to write a summary.

### Differentiation

If the content of the reading is completely unfamiliar to ELLs, build their prior knowledge and vocabulary for the topic. Students reading below grade level may have trouble identifying the phrases to sort, so scaffold the task by completing some of the strips for the students. Gifted students can extend the activity by writing a summary based on how they categorized the phrases.

# Summarizing Strategies for Mathematics (cont.)

## Rank-Ordering Retell (cont.)

### Grades 1–2 Example

| **Most important ideas:** |
| --- |
| Addition and subtraction are related to each other within fact families. |
| **Moderately important ideas:** |
| For example: 8 + 4 = 12; 4 + 8 = 12; 12 − 4 = 8; and 12 − 8 = 4. |
| **Least important ideas:** |
| There are often multiple fact families for a number.  For example, 6 + 6 = 12 and 12 − 6 = 6 are also a fact family for 12. |

### Grades 3–5 Example

| **Most important ideas:** |
| --- |
| Multiplication and division are inversely related to each other. |
| **Moderately important ideas:** |
| For example: 3 x 4 = 12; 4 x 3 = 12; and 12 ÷ 4 = 3; 12 ÷ 3 = 4. |
| **Least important ideas:** |
| There are often multiple inverse relationships for the same product. For example, 2 x 6 = 12; 12 ÷ 2 = 6 |

### Grades 6–8 Example

| **Most important ideas:** |
| --- |
| Slope determines the steepness of a linear function. |
| **Moderately important ideas:** |
| A positive slope indicates that the line will go upward, and a negative slope indicates that the line will go downward. |
| **Least important ideas:** |
| Slope is often represented by the letter *m* when it is an unknown variable. |

**Name:** _____

# Rank-Ordering Retell

**Directions:** On separate slips of paper, write down important phrases from the text. Then sort the strips into these three categories: most important ideas, moderately important ideas, and least important ideas.

**Most important ideas:**

**Moderately important ideas:**

**Least important ideas:**

# Summarizing Strategies for Mathematics *(cont.)*

## GIST

### Background Information

As the name suggests, students use GIST (Moore, Moore, Cunningham, and Cunningham 1994) to explain the "gist" of what they have read by writing a very concise and precise summary. The goal is to write a summary of 20 words or less. Students use revision techniques until their summaries are 20 words are less. As with other summarizing activities, GIST forces students to eliminate extraneous details and determine what is most important in the reading. When introducing GIST, it is important to discuss the characteristics and qualities of a good summary. Teachers remind students to eliminate unnecessary information and delete any redundancies. Teachers ask the students to locate the main ideas and the most important information. Students also generalize details and lists by using broad categories that encompass the details and items on the lists. They locate the topic sentences of each paragraph or create their own topic sentences in order to convey the information of each paragraph. They also use key words and phrases to relay the information to the reader. Good summaries are also revised so that they sound natural.

### Grade Levels/Standards Addressed

Grades 6–8 (Standard 7.3)

### Activity

Provide students with a section of mathematics text that is no more than three paragraphs long and is easy to read. Ask them to read the paragraphs silently. Tell them that as they read, they should pay attention to the important ideas in the passage. When the students are finished reading, distribute the GIST strategy sheet (page 154). Then ask students to name the important ideas and write these on the board or on an overhead transparency. As a class, work together to condense the information into 20 words or less.

### Extension

Ask the students to read a second section of text that is also three paragraphs long. Have the students create a new 20-word summary that includes the information from both reading selections. Allow students to repeat the process with a third section when they are very comfortable with the procedures.

### Differentiation

While completing the summary with the whole class during the modeling phase, it is important to slow down your speech and use simple vocabulary so that ELLs can follow along. Find ways to rephrase and repeat what you are saying to help ELLs understand the process better and be sure to check for their understanding. Students reading below grade level should work with a partner rather than independently to locate the important ideas and words. Challenge gifted students by assigning them longer or denser reading selections to summarize. Also, limit their summaries to 15 words.

## GIST *(cont.)*

### Grades 6–8 Example

**Important Ideas from Section 1:**

rational _____     repeating pattern _____     pi (π) _____

irrational _____     decimal _____     _____

real number _____     fraction _____     _____

**Summary:**

Rational numbers can be written as a fraction, a terminating decimal, or a repeating decimal. Irrational numbers are those that cannot be written as a fraction. As a decimal, they do not repeat or terminate. The fraction $\frac{1}{2}$ is a rational number, but pi (π) is an irrational number. Both rational and irrational numbers are considered real numbers.

**Condensed Summary:**

Rational numbers, like $\frac{1}{2}$ or 2.5, are fractions or terminating or repeating decimals. Irrational numbers, like pi (π), do not terminate as decimals.

**Name:** _____

# GIST

**Directions:** After reading the first section of a text, write down the important ideas and create a summary. Then read the second section of text and write down the important ideas. Condense all the information into a combined summary.

**Important Ideas from Section 1:**

_____    _____    _____

_____    _____    _____

_____    _____    _____

_____    _____    _____

**Summary:**

_____

_____

_____

**Condensed Summary:**

_____

_____

_____

# Summarizing Strategies for Mathematics *(cont.)*

## Key Words

### Background Information

Key Words (Hoyt 2002) works in much the same way as GIST, but it is designed to be used with younger students and does not limit the number of words in the summary. In this strategy, after students have read a short selection of text, they are asked to identify one word that is most important—the "key word"—to summarize the selection. As students continue reading the selection, they generate a list of words that they can use to create a written or oral summary. The strategy is effective because it helps students locate the most important concepts (words), encourages them to use their own words, and forces them to spend more time reading and processing the information.

### Grade Levels/Standards Addressed

Grades 1–2 (Standard 7.3)
Grades 3–5 (Standard 7.5)

### Activity

Select a section of text for the students to read that is fairly short. Distribute sticky notes, small sheets of paper, or notebook paper. Ask students to read the selection carefully (or conduct a read-aloud or choral reading with primary students) to locate the most important words to summarize the information. Instruct them to write down the most important words in the selection as they read.

When the students have finished, collect the words or ask the students to share the words they selected with the entire class. Make a list of the students' words. Discuss the value of each word and ask the students to explain and justify their choices to the class. Demonstrate how to construct a summary based on the words students have chosen. Show students how to combine information, eliminate redundancies, and use their own words so that the summary sounds natural. Introduce the list of transition words (page 156) for students to use when constructing their summaries. When students understand the procedure, gradually release the responsibility to them by placing them in pairs to complete the task. With practice, the students will use the strategy automatically as they process the text and summarize for clarification.

### Differentiation

While ELLs may not struggle to identify the key words in a reading selection, they may struggle to incorporate the words into a cohesive summary. Pair ELLs with other students to work together to create the summary. Students reading below grade level may need the activity scaffolded for them. Select some key words for the students when they are working independently so that they can focus their attention when locating other words. Gifted students should be given reading materials that are appropriate for their reading levels.

## Key Words *(cont.)*

### Common Transition Words for Summarizing

Using transitions in summaries helps the text read more naturally, allowing the ideas to flow smoothly in a coherent manner.

| **Generalizing** | | | |
|---|---|---|---|
| generally | generally speaking | usually | ordinarily |
| as a rule | as usual | for the most part | |

| **Adding Details** | | | |
|---|---|---|---|
| also | besides | furthermore | in addition |
| moreover | again | in fact | for this reason |
| for example | for instance | and | next |
| finally | another | such as | |

| **Comparing and Contrasting** | | | |
|---|---|---|---|
| in contrast | instead | likewise | on one hand |
| on the other hand | on the contrary | rather | similarly |
| yet | however | still | nevertheless |
| neither/nor | but | both | instead |

| **Sequencing** | | | |
|---|---|---|---|
| at first | first of all | to begin with | in the first place |
| at the same time | for now | for the time being | the next step |
| next | in time | in turn | later on |
| meanwhile | then | soon | later |
| while | earlier | simultaneously | afterward |
| in the end | in conclusion | | |

# Summarizing Srategies for Mathematics *(cont.)*

## Very Important Points

### Background Information

Identifying the main idea and the most important points in a reading selection is integral to summarizing. Students are often expected to summarize without receiving any explicit instruction on how to do so. Teachers need to model how to gather information prior to writing a summary. In the Very Important Points (VIP) strategy (Hoyt 2002), students place sticky strips on the text to indicate the most important ideas. The tactile or kinesthetic action of placing sticky strips onto the pages of the book increases student involvement and motivation. Students can also use the sticky strips to identify points of interest, points of confusion, precise details, a place where the student makes a connection—whatever the teacher or the students wish to focus on. Students then discuss the VIPs they select either with partners, in small groups, or as a whole class. They can use the VIPs to help them summarize the reading selection. Students also like the flexibility of the sticky strips. After discussion, they can change their minds and move the sticky strips if they wish, which boosts their confidence.

### Grade Levels/Standards Addressed

Grades 1–2 (Standard 7.3)
Grades 3–5 (Standard 7.5)
Grades 6–8 (Standard 7.3)

### Activity

Select a section of the text for students to read. Determine in advance the number of VIPs that students can identify as they read the selection. Distribute the set number of sticky strips (sticky notes that have been cut into thin strips of paper with a sticky end) to students. Clearly establish the purpose for reading and explain to students what they will be looking for as they read (the most important ideas, unnecessary information, precise details, points of interest, points of confusion, a place that triggers a connection, etc.). Instruct students to place the sticky strips directly on the text. After reading, have students meet with partners or in small groups to discuss the VIPs they selected. Students should then explain and justify their choices and take notes. They may move their sticky strips if they choose.

### Variation

To make the task more challenging, require the students in the small groups to come to a consensus about the location of the sticky strips in a section. Ask students to justify their choices with evidence from the text.

### Differentiation

Give ELLs adequate time to prepare for defending their sticky note placement. Students reading below grade level will benefit from limiting the number of sticky strips assigned to them. Otherwise, they may use too many sticky notes. Gifted students should be asked to use the sticky strips for a more complex task, such as identifying moments that trigger a connection. Encourage them to explore the connections in greater depth.

# Summarizing Strategies for Mathematics *(cont.)*

## Guided Reading and Summarizing Procedure

### Background Information

Transforming the information provided in a reading selection by compressing it into a synopsis is a challenge for many students. The Guided Reading and Summarizing Procedure (GRASP) (Lenski, Wham, and Johns 1999) enables students to summarize independently. The strategy helps to increase students' abilities to recall information, self-correct, and organize materials.

### Grade Levels/Standards Addressed

Grades 3–5 (Standard 7.5)
Grades 6–8 (Standard 7.3)

### Activity

Provide a mathematics selection to the students. Tell students that they are going to be learning how to summarize what they have read. Explain when summarizing is a useful tool. Direct students to read the selection with the purpose of trying to remember all they can. After they have finished reading, ask them to tell you what they remember without looking at the text. List the items on the board or on an overhead transparency. Instruct students to reread the selection to see if there is any other information that should be included on the list. The students should also check the list to correct any incorrect information. Next, evaluate the list as a class to identify the main ideas of the passage and group the information on the list accordingly. Using the organizational structure created by categorizing the information, write a summary of the material in the category as a whole class and model the process for the students. Instruct students to omit unnecessary information, combine as much information as possible, and add

information to make the summary read naturally and coherently. Ryder and Graves (2003) suggest that the students and the teacher write the summary for the next category individually and compare and contrast the students' summaries to that of the teacher. Ryder and Graves (2003) point out that Hayes (1989) suggests the teacher revise his or her summary based on the students' alternatives and make a visible record of these changes so the revision process is more concrete for the students. As students continue to summarize each category, model the revision process in great detail. When students learn how to conduct GRASP independently, they can use the handout (page 161) to help them construct their summaries independently.

### Differentiation

ELLs should have the text available to them during the "remembering the information" stage of the activity. Students reading below grade level may need someone to read the passage aloud, rephrase sections, and provide explanations. Both ELLs and students reading below grade level should work with partners or in small groups to remember the information and construct the summary. Gifted students may not benefit from the instruction and modeling phase of the activity and can be encouraged to work independently.

## Guided Reading and Summarizing Procedure (cont.)

**Grades 3–5 Example**

| Details Remembered from Reading | Additions/Corrections |
|---|---|
| Square pyramids have 5 faces. | Cylinders have 2 faces. |
| 4 of a square pyramid's faces are triangles and 1 is a square. | The faces of a cylinder are circles. |
| Square pyramids have 8 edges. | Cylinders have no vertices. |
| Square pyramids have 5 vertices. | Cubes have 6 faces. |
| Rectangular prisms have 6 faces. | The faces of a cube are all squares. |
| The faces of a rectangular prisms are either rectangles or squares. | Cubes have 12 edges. |
| Rectangular prisms have 12 edges. | Cubes have 8 vertices. |
| Rectangular prisms have 8 vertices. | Cubes are also rectangular prisms. |
| Cones have 1 vertex. | |
| Spheres have no faces. | |
| Spheres have no edges. | |
| Spheres have no vertices. | |

| Main Ideas in Reading |
|---|
| Three-dimensional shapes can be compared by counting faces, edges, and vertices. |
| The faces of three-dimensional shapes are made of regular plane shapes. |

# Summarizing Strategies for Mathematics (cont.)

## Guided Reading and Summarizing Procedure (cont.)

### Grades 6–8 Example

| Details Remembered from Reading | Additions/Corrections |
|---|---|
| F.O.I.L. stands for First, Outer, Inner, Last. | The result of the process is a trinomial. |
| When multiplying 2 binomials, you start by multiplying the first term of the first binomial by the first term of the second binomial. | The first term of the trinomial often has a squared variable. |
| Then you multiply the first term of the first binomial and the second term of the second binomial. | The second term of the trinomial often has a single variable. |
| Then you multiply the second term of the first binomial by the first term of the second binomial. | The last term is usually a constant. |
| Finally, you multiply the second term of the first binomial by the second term of the second binomial. | |
| After performing the F.O.I.L. method, you have to combine the two terms in the middle into one term. | |

| Main Ideas in Reading |
|---|
| F.O.I.L. is a method for simplifying two binomials into a single trinomial. |
| There are four steps to executing the F.O.I.L. method. |

**Name:** _____

# Guided Reading and Summarizing Procedure

**Directions:** After reading a selected text, write down what you remember in the top left section. Then reread the text and write down any additional information in the top right section. Finally, evaluate the list and identify the main ideas and details to create an effective summary in the bottom section.

| Details Remembered from Reading | Additions/Corrections |
|---|---|
|  |  |

| Main Ideas in Reading |
|---|
|  |

# Using Visual Representations of Text and Mental Imagery in Mathematics

## Teaching Visual Representations

There are three aspects to how visual representations of text are involved in reading comprehension. Teaching visual representations of text can be accomplished by direct instruction of how to construct mental images during reading. Teaching students to create pictures in their minds as they read improves their reading comprehension. Another aspect involves teaching students how to read, evaluate, and construct the visual material that accompanies informational text. In addition, visual representations of text can take the form of flow charts, mind maps, concept maps, Venn diagrams, etc. One method for students to process reading materials is through the assistance of accompanying graphic organizers. This section focuses on how to use mental imagery to improve reading comprehension, and also addresses teaching students how to evaluate and create visual materials.

## Mental Imagery

The ability to create mental images while reading is called *visualization*. When readers visualize what they have read in mental images, they create a framework for organizing and remembering the text (Gambrell and Koskinen 2002). In this framework, key images work as triggers for memory storage and retrieval. Several research studies on mental imagery construction demonstrate that the strategy increases readers' memory for text that they visualized and improves their identification of inconsistencies in the reading material (Gambrell and Koskinen 2002). These studies show that mental imagery is integral to improving listening and reading comprehension.

## Active Processing

Recent researchers have determined that when students make mental images, they engage in an active information-handling process (Gambrell and Koskinen 2002). Engaging in the text through mental imagery promotes the active processing of the text because the reader must construct meaningful images that link prior knowledge with the information in the text. Researchers are not exactly sure why visualization works as a reading comprehension strategy, but they speculate that when readers construct mental images, they are processing both visual images and print. This causes the reader to put forth greater effort and results in the reader processing the text in much greater depth. As a result of using mental imagery, readers increase their ability to actively integrate the information they learn from the text into their memories. Therefore, using mental images to comprehend text promotes more involved, active processing in readers.

# Using Visual Representations of Text and Mental Imagery in Mathematics *(cont.)*

## Some Benefits of Visualization

Some of the reasons to teach students to evoke mental images while reading are as follows (Keene and Zimmerman 1997):

- In order to create mental images, students must use all five senses and their emotions, which are linked to their prior knowledge.

- Creating images immerses students in a wealth of rich details. The details are compelling, memorable, and leave a stronger impression of the text.

- Readers who adapt their mental images in response to other readers' mental images are considered more proficient.

## Other Benefits of Imagery

Mental imagery can facilitate students in their writing. Creating mental images when reading, developing ideas, and working out details promotes reflection and contemplation. More reflection and contemplation by the writer results in better writing.

Imagery construction also promotes inference skills. Students must infer information provided in their reading as well as in the images they construct or that they view. When students are skilled at using inference as a reading comprehension strategy, they are more strategic readers.

While there is no real evidence to establish that using imagery enhances motivation to read, Gambrell and Koskinen (2002) suggest that imagery positively affects motivation. They cite a study by Long, Winograd, and Bridge (1989) that found the strength of the images (vividness) was related to reading interest.

## Comprehension Monitoring

Using mental imagery also helps readers to monitor their comprehension. Gambrell and Koskinen (2002) cite an earlier study by Gambrell and Bales (1986) in which the evidence demonstrated that students who were encouraged to construct mental images while reading performed significantly better at the comprehension-monitoring task than those who did not. Imagery is considered a particularly effective strategy for poor readers because producing images helps them process the text with greater depth.

# Using Visual Representations of Text and Mental Imagery in Mathematics *(cont.)*

## Steps to Build Imagery Competence and Confidence in Students

Teachers can engage in the following sequence of activities with students to build their skills and confidence in imagery construction (Fredericks 1986; Barclay 1990, as cited by Gambrell and Koskinen 2002):

1. **Provide opportunities for students to create images of concrete objects.** Have students look carefully at an object, such as a rectangular prism, close their eyes, and form a mental picture of the object. Encourage students to compare and contrast their mental images with the actual object.

2. **Provide opportunities for guided imagery of concrete objects.** For example, have the students make a mental picture of a football field. The teacher should provide guided imagery by refining the picture. *There is green grass and the sun is shining. There is a goalpost at either end of the field. There is a dirt track that goes around the entire field. Imagine running around the track. You are in a race with your best friend. You are running the perimeter of the field.*

3. **Encourage students to imagine pictures in their minds and recall familiar objects or scenes.** The teacher might ask the students to create a mental picture of their kitchens and then draw a picture of what it looks like. They can then apply a scale to the drawing and calculate the area of the picture. They could then take the drawing home and measure their own kitchens and compare their visualizations to the actual room.

4. **Provide guided instruction to support students in making images of events and actions.** Teachers may begin by asking students to imagine a concrete object (a bear at one side of a large lake), but then expand the guided imagery to include movement and action. *The bear looks to the other side of the rushing water, where he sees a tree with a beehive full of honey. He enters the rushing water. The lake is 200 feet across, but he swims as fast as he can. It only takes him 15 minutes to swim across the lake. He climbs the tall, 20-foot tree in 3 minutes, swipes the beehive, and gets his honey.*

5. **Develop the use of imagery in listening situations.** For example, when reading how to gather, measure, and compare information from a table or graph, the teacher can conduct a guided imagery of a the table or graph. *The first thing I notice is that Palm Springs had the highest temperature for the month of August—115 degrees. Imagine how hot that would feel. Even the swimming pools would be hot. The next hottest city…*

6. **Provide instructions to students to create their own mental images as they read.** When students read text with illustrations, encourage them to focus on the illustrations and use them to make their own images of the information in the text. *Look at the graph of the different speeds of the cars during the race. The shape of the graph looks like a hill. If I remember that image as I answer the questions about the graph, I will already have estimated an answer.*

# Using Visual Representations of Text and Mental Imagery in Mathematics *(cont.)*

## Teaching Students to Create Mental Images

Not all teachers feel comfortable with teaching imagery as a comprehension strategy. The skills involved in creating and instructing with Guided Imagery activities, for example, involve a great deal of creativity. In addition, students may not have engaged in any image-constructing activities in their schooling and may feel somewhat inhibited at first. However, the strategy is extremely effective with students because it helps them to "see" in their mind's eye what it is that they are reading. Once they have mastered the strategy, it becomes second nature. Developing mental image construction skills in students can make reading as natural as watching a movie.

Teachers must model mental image construction for the students and provide detailed explanations about generating mental images. The most effective technique to do this is through the Think-Aloud strategy. Teachers verbalize their thoughts about how they construct and use imagery while reading a passage aloud to students. As students become more comfortable with their teacher's imagery, they are encouraged to expand on the teacher's images. Gradually, the students are invited to share their own images, and when ready, they are guided to expand on their own images.

The key to developing this skill, as with other reading strategies, is to provide the students with many opportunities to share their images. Teachers and the students can help each other to better describe their images. And, because mental images are visual representations of words and ideas, it is important to allow the students to draw and illustrate their own mental pictures of their reading materials. Sharing their own drawings, explaining them, defending their choices, and comparing them to other illustrations allows for greater understanding of the content in the text.

## Some Tips for Using Imagery

Gambrell and Koskinen (2002) suggest the following general guidelines for using imagery:

- Remind students that everyone's images are unique. Students should be encouraged to accept and respect different perspectives. Their prior experience will determine what images they create.

- Encourage students to use the clues in the reading and their background knowledge to form appropriate images to help them understand what they are reading. There are no right or wrong answers when creating images, but students must rely on inference and prior knowledge to be on the right track.

- Use read-alouds so students can create images as they listen. Gradually release the responsibility to the students so they can picture the content of the reading in their minds when they read independently.

# Using Visual Representations of Text and Mental Imagery in Mathematics *(cont.)*

## How Imagery Is Linked to Visuals

Some of the most important features included in most mathematics informational texts are visual representations. Photographs, illustrations, drawings, flowcharts, diagrams, graphs, and maps are common in textbooks today because they capture the attention of the reader. Examining visuals is an important skill to develop because the visuals contain so much information. Struggling readers need the information provided by visuals to assist them as they decode the text. If instructed to do so, they can learn how to use clues from the visuals to help them to better understand what they are reading. Furthermore, reading researchers have determined that readers who are able to combine their ability to generate mental imagery with attending to illustrations provided in a text better understand what they are reading (Gambrell and Jawitz 1993).

Hoyt (2002) suggests that students should be instructed to analyze visuals that accompany informational text. They should be able to examine the size of photographs, the placement on the page, the caption or title, etc. In essence, it is useful to teach students the elements of layout so that they can develop an awareness of how the layout contributes to the overall reading experience and their ability to comprehend the text.

It is important to heighten the reader's awareness of the visuals because "they make the information come alive" (Hoyt 2002, p. 136). Teachers bring the visuals into focus for the students so they can better understand how visuals support the text, how the visuals affect the reader, etc. As Hoyt (2002) points out, many students, particularly those who are not proficient readers, have a tendency to ignore the pictures and diagrams that accompany the text. The task of reading is so arduous for them that they cannot waste time looking at the visuals when they read. These visuals are present to make the job of reading easier for them, so teachers must use visual representations in text as a reading comprehension strategy in the mathematics classroom.

## Quick and Easy Activities with Visuals:

- Provide students with a variety of visuals that could possibly accompany the reading. Ask them to invent the captions for the visuals. In doing so, the students will synthesize and summarize key concepts and main ideas in a highly condensed form.

- Provide students with informational text with no accompanying visuals, and ask them to invent the visuals for the textbook or magazine. Have them consider the best size, location on the page, etc. to make the article more inviting and informative.

- Have students create comic strips about the content of the reading. Have them work together to explain information in a sequence. Adding humor helps students engage in the activity.

- Introduce new concepts with a picture book. Many mathematics teachers at the middle and high school levels have found that using picture books designed for much younger readers helps older students retain new information. Picture books help activate prior knowledge before reading and prepare the students' schemas for adding new information.

# Visual Representations of Text and Mental Imagery Strategies for Mathematics

## Guided Imagery

## Background Information

Guided Imagery is a comprehension strategy that has a long history in reading, language arts, and social studies classes but is rarely, if ever, used in mathematics. Using the technique, teachers can help students create mental images to anticipate or respond to what they read or hear. Teachers should spend ample time preparing a script for the Guided Imagery strategy by developing an analogy or metaphor that appropriately depicts the concept. These scripts can be presented to the class either before or after completing the reading. To develop the script, teachers expand the analogy to appeal to the five senses in the hopes of increasing the vividness of the experience for the students. When the activity is completed, teachers discuss and reinforce with the students how creating these images can enhance reading comprehension and remembering the concepts in the reading.

### Grade Levels/Standards Addressed

Grades 1–2 (Standard 5.1)
Grades 3–5 (Standard 5.2)
Grades 6–8 (Standard 5.2)

## Activity

After students have developed some skill in mental image construction, introduce the Guided Imagery script (see samples on page 168). Put a note on the classroom door to prevent interruptions, turn off the classroom lights, and close the curtains or blinds.

Ask students to get comfortable (they may wish to sit on the floor), close their eyes, relax as much as possible, and listen carefully as you read the script. Suggest the image one sentence at a time and speak slowly, but clearly. Repeat words and phrases, and pause periodically to allow students the opportunity to develop and expand the images they are creating. When you have finished the script, allow the students to "wake up" slowly. Ask them to describe and explain their images. Ask students to tell what they heard, saw, and felt. It may help to have the students complete a quick-write prior to sharing with the class to facilitate a more lively discussion. During the discussion, point out the similarities between their images and the content of the reading selection.

## Differentiation

Be sure to speak slowly and enunciate clearly while reading the script to help ELLs understand your words. Make sure the vocabulary and content of the script are not too complex for students reading below grade level. Write the script for students reading below grade level, but elaborate for gifted students.

# Visual Representations of Text and Mental Imagery Strategies for Mathematics (cont.)

## Guided Imagery (cont.)

### Grades 1–2 Example
**Concepts of Time**

"Close your eyes and imagine that you are lying in bed. You feel the warmth of the covers and the soft pillow under your head. You open your eyes and see that the sun is just barely peeking into your room. It is morning and you realize that there are many things to do in the morning. You get out of bed and put a robe and slippers on. You walk to the bathroom and wash your face. You brush your teeth and comb your hair. You hear your mom. What is she saying? You listen carefully, and you hear her say, 'It's time for breakfast!' You run downstairs and smell bacon, pancakes, and sweet maple syrup. This is your favorite part of the morning—BREAKFAST! When your tummy is all full, you head back upstairs to get dressed. You are ready for the next part of the day."

### Grades 3–5 Example
**Solving Problems with Addition and Multiplication**

"Close your eyes and imagine that you and your 3 best friends are standing in line at your favorite pizza place. Your stomach is growling and you have been imagining the gooey, yummy cheese of a warm pizza all day. You know that you are going to eat at least 3 pieces of pizza. You and your friends have all decided to get extra cheese and pepperoni. You ask your friends how many pieces they each want. One wants 3 pieces. One wants 2 pieces and one wants 5 pieces. With your 3 pieces, you wonder how many pieces that makes. That would be 3 plus 3, which is 6; plus 2, which is 8; plus 5, which is 13. But the large pizza has only 12 pieces. You would have to buy two large pizzas, which would give you 24 slices. That is too much! You

look at the menu and the prices on the wall. A small pizza is 6 slices. A medium pizza is 8 slices. You don't know what to do. What if we bought 2 small pizzas? That would be 6 times 2, which makes 12. That won't work. What if we bought 2 medium pizzas, which would be 8 times 2, or 16 pieces. That would be enough, but not as much as two large pizzas. That is what we will do!"

### Grades 6–8 Example
**Ratios**

"Close your eyes and imagine that you have just gotten off the bus at summer camp. You look around and notice that there are many buses. You wonder how many kids there are at summer camp with you. There seem to be a lot. First, you think that if you count the buses and then count the number of kids on one bus, then you could multiply the number of buses by the number of kids. But wait! Some of the buses are big and some are small. In fact, there are 3 or 4 different size buses. The camp counselors tell you to gather around them, and it seems like there must be hundreds of kids around you. You cannot figure out how many kids there are. Your lead camp counselor says that you are going to be divided into tribes and assigned to cabins. For every 1 cabin, there will be 12 kids. Hey—that is a ratio of 1 to 12. You are curious, so you raise your hand and ask, 'Excuse me, how many cabins are there total?' Your camp counselor says that there are 10 cabins total. You quickly think to yourself. If there is a ratio of 1 cabin to 12 kids, then 10 cabins would accommodate 120 kids. You yell out, 'That means there are as many as 120 kids at camp here.' Your camp counselor smiles and remarks on what great math skills you have. Camp is off to a great start."

# Visual Representations of Text and Mental Imagery Strategies for Mathematics *(cont.)*

## Talking Drawings

### Background Information

One way to activate students' prior knowledge and generate interest on a topic is through the Talking Drawings activity (McConnell 1993, as cited by Wood 2002). Research shows that motivating students to create images before, during, and after reading is an effective method for improving reading comprehension. Prior to reading in the Talking Drawings activity, students create a mental picture initiated by the teacher. They draw what they imagined, and they share their drawings with the entire class. The teacher compiles all of the information of the sharing in a semantic map on the board or an overhead transparency. After reading the selection using the mental images they created while they read, students repeat the process and discuss what they have learned after comparing and contrasting the two pictures. All students, but particularly emergent learners, benefit from being provided a way to express their ideas in another way.

### Grade Levels/Standards Addressed

Grades 1–2 (Standards 5.1, 7.4)
Grades 3–5 (Standard 7.6)

### Activity

Instruct students to close their eyes and allow their minds to form mental pictures on a topic you have selected. For example, if the selected topic is *fractions*, students might picture a pizza or cake cut into equal parts. When students are finished picturing, ask them to draw what they see, using labels to depict parts, locations, people involved, and so on as necessary. After drawing, place students in pairs to share their drawings and talk about what they drew and why. Encourage them to ask their partners questions about their drawings. Meet as a whole class and use a transparency to gather all of the information students generated in the Talking Drawings semantic map (page 172). Instruct students to read the reading selection with their pictures in mind. After reading, ask them to make another drawing to show what they have learned. Then have them discuss their pictures with their partners and ask questions about their partners' pictures.

### Differentiation

ELLs should be encouraged to label their first picture in their native language. They can add the words in English later. Students reading below grade level should be placed in homogenous groups to reduce anxiety. Gifted students may have nothing to write during the writing task, so provide them with a reflective question.

# Visual Representations of Text and Mental Imagery Strategies for Mathematics *(cont.)*

## Talking Drawings *(cont.)*

**Grades 1–2 Example**

| **Before Reading** | Close your eyes and think about the topic. Draw what you see. Talk about your drawing with your partner. |
|---|---|

| **After Reading** | Read the selection and then draw a new picture of what you learned. |
|---|---|

| **What's Different?** | Explain what is different about your before and after pictures. |
|---|---|

My first picture has only a circle, a square, and a triangle. My second picture has a lot more shapes because I learned more shapes. I learned about rectangles, ovals, diamonds, and that even a heart is a shape.

# Visual Representations of Text and Mental Imagery Strategies for Mathematics *(cont.)*

## Talking Drawings *(cont.)*

**Grades 3–5 Example**

| Before Reading | Close your eyes and think about the topic. Draw what you see. Talk about your drawing with your partner. |
|---|---|

| 1, | 5 | 6 | 7 |
|---|---|---|---|
| one thousand | five hundreds | six tens | seven ones |

| After Reading | Read the selection and then draw a new picture of what you learned. |
|---|---|

| 1, | 2 | 7 | 8, | 5 | 6 | 3 |
|---|---|---|---|---|---|---|
| one million | two hundred thousands | seven ten thousands | eight thousands | five hundreds | six tens | three ones |

| What's Different? | Explain what is different about your before and after pictures. |
|---|---|

Before I read more about place value, I already knew the ones place, tens place, hundreds place, and thousands place. Now I have learned past the thousands place all the way to the millions place.

**Name:** _____

# Talking Drawings

| **Before Reading** | Close your eyes and think about the topic. Draw what you see. Talk about your drawing with your partner. |
|---|---|
| | |
| **After Reading** | Read the selection and then draw a new picture of what you learned. |
| | |
| **What's Different?** | Explain what is different about your before and after pictures. |
| | |

# Visual Representations of Text and Mental Imagery Strategies for Mathematics (cont.)

## Imagine, Elaborate, Predict, and Confirm

### Background Information

Imagine, Elaborate, Predict, and Confirm (IEPC) is a mental imagery strategy combined with prediction that helps students comprehend text better and improve the details in their writing. It requires students to use their imaginations as they predict and confirm what they will be reading. The IEPC strategy has been field tested and has proven to increase motivation and interest, in addition to improving comprehension and writing skills (Wood 2002).

In the *imagine phase*, the teacher asks students to close their eyes and use their imaginations to create pictures about the reading selection. The teacher can direct the students to formulate their pictures based on the book cover, title, pictures, etc. Students are encouraged to use all of their senses during this phase. The teacher then writes everything that students report on an IEPC transparency.

In the *elaboration phase*, students expand on their original images by using prior knowledge and adding details. By sharing their pictures with the whole class, the students may stimulate one another to describe more.

Students make simple predictions based on their images during the *prediction phase*. They are then instructed to keep their predictions in mind as they complete the reading task.

During the *confirmation stage*, students return to their predictions and determine whether they were correct. The teacher and the students modify the original predictions and integrate the new information learned.

### Grade Levels/Standards Addressed

Grades 1–2 (Standard 5.2)
Grades 3–5 (Standard 5.3)
Grades 6–8 (Standard 5.1)

### Activity

Instruct students to close their eyes and try to picture everything they can on the topic. Encourage them to use all of their senses to experience the images. Ask them to report on their mental images and record these on an IEPC transparency (page 174) for the class to review. Next, model how to add more details and information to their visual images and record this on the transparency. Encourage students to follow your lead. Again, using the think-aloud technique, make at least one prediction about what you expect to find in the reading based on the visual images, and ask students to do the same. Ask students to complete the reading task. After reading, have students review their predictions to see if they were correct. Model how to revise the predictions and integrate them with the new information being learned. It is important to model exactly how to go back to the text and locate the key parts to check predictions.

### Differentiation

ELLs will be able to comprehend the reading selection better if it is read aloud to them as they follow along with the printed material in front of them. Students reading below grade level may prefer to conduct the reading in pairs and summarize or retell sections to partners, while gifted students may prefer to read silently.

**Name:** _____

# Imagine, Elaborate, Predict, and Confirm

| Imagine | Elaborate |
|---------|-----------|
|         |           |

**Predict**

_____

_____

**Confirm**

_____

_____

*Adapted from Karen Wood "Differentiating Reading and Writing Lessons to Promote Content Learning" (pp. 164–165)*

# Visual Representations of Text and Mental Imagery Strategies for Mathematics *(cont.)*

## Sketching Through Text

### Background Information

Sketching is a type of informal illustration that can be used as a classroom activity to help students illustrate and support ideas (Hoyt 2002). In order to model how sketching can be used, teachers should frequently sketch on the board. During mathematics read-alouds, teachers should stop and think aloud to review what they have just learned and then make a quick sketch on the board to show what information has been learned. The sketches do not need to be done perfectly—stick figures work very well. Hoyt (2002) encourages teachers to explore different ways to express ideas in sketches. Teachers can use arrows to indicate the passage of time. Some sketches may be linear, others circular. Some sketches can take the form of graphic organizers. Interestingly, students can sketch in the same way that they can write: to show what they are learning and to solidify their understandings. However, when students write about what they have learned, they do not actively engage in its contents when presenting it to others; they just read it aloud. In contrast, when students present their sketches to a partner or the rest of the class, they have yet another opportunity to talk about and process what they have learned. This promotes greater retention and revision.

### Grade Levels/Standards Addressed

Grades 1–2 (Standard 7.3)
Grades 3–5 (Standard 7.5)
Grades 6–8 (Standard 7.3)

### Activity

Select a passage in the textbook that accommodates a sketching activity, e.g., parts of the whole or two- and three-dimensional shapes. Distribute copies of the Sketching Through Text handout (page 176). Ask students to identify the most important points in the reading passage, and have them give each main idea a name. Tell them to illustrate the main points on the handout. Place students in pairs or small groups to share their sketches with one another. The students should explain and justify their selections and describe their sketches. When the students are finished, meet as a whole class and ask each group to present and explain a main point that someone in their group identified and justified well. To promote greater self-monitoring skills, make sure to ask the students to explain how sketching helps them as readers and whether it helps them learn better.

### Differentiation

ELLs may not be able to understand the textbook well, so it may be necessary to provide them with a reading selection appropriate for them. Students reading below grade level may benefit from working with partners during the illustrating phase. Make sure that students below grade level present their ideas to the class during the whole-class discussion, as this will include them more in the discussion. Gifted students should be prompted to explain their selections to model their critical thinking skills.

# Sketching Through Text

**Directions:** After reading the text, identify the most important points and give each a name. Then illustrate the main points in the boxes below.

|  |  |
|---|---|
|  |  |
|  |  |
|  |  |

# Visual Representations of Text and Mental Imagery Strategies for Mathematics (cont.)

## Visual Presentations

### Background Information

It is important for teachers who are trying to develop visual representation activities to teach and model the strategy in a variety of ways. Visual Presentations (Hoyt 2002) is a strategy that combines both mental imaging and the production of visuals for presentation purposes. In addition, the strategy helps students locate the main idea and generalize information as if they were summarizing. Teachers begin by modeling how to select a presentation format that works best for the information in the text. Teachers may need to explain different presentation formats to the students at this time. Students must then select the format that works best for the reading selection that they have independently chosen. Next, students read the selection, and based on their reading, they plan out visual presentations of what they have read. After the students have finished, they should discuss their visuals to enhance their understanding of the text even further.

### Grade Levels/Standards Addressed

Grades 1–2 (Standard 7.3)
Grades 3–5 (Standard 7.5)
Grades 6–8 (Standard 7.3)

### Activity

Assign students a selection of text to read that includes many visual aids (charts, illustrations, diagrams, maps, photos, captions). Have them read the selection and discuss how they could visually represent the text and why. Use questioning and discussion to help students see that there are multiple ways to represent the text visually. Have the students discuss what visual representation would work best to embody the information. Prompt the students through guided questioning as needed. For example, when reading about a survey or other statistical information, discuss what visual representation would work best (pie graph or bar graph). Allow them to work in small groups to develop a visual presentation of the text. When the students are finished, have the groups share their presentations with the class.

### Variation

When the students have demonstrated that they can create visual presentations independently, have them do a jigsaw of visual presentations as a review tool. Break up a long section of text that the students have read and ask the different groups to create visual presentations of their section of the text. Each group presents their visual presentation in order to review the reading more thoroughly.

### Differentiation

ELLs may struggle to present their visual presentations to the class, so be sure to provide them with adequate time to prepare. Students reading below grade level should be asked to create a visual presentation for a shorter selection of the text. Gifted students should be encouraged to use their ideas for the visual presentations as possible advertising posters that can be hung up in the school library.

# Visual Representations of Text and Mental Imagery Strategies for Mathematics *(cont.)*

## Examining Visuals

### Background Information

Another way teachers can work to improve their students' ability to comprehend printed text is to teach them how to analyze the visuals included in the text. Taking a closer look at the visuals in nonfiction mathematics texts helps students focus on the key concepts, find the main idea, highlight important details, learn additional information that is not included in the text, and expand their understanding of the content. It is best to introduce this strategy with a mathematics selection that contains a lot of visuals (graphs, images, tables, etc.). Model for the students in a think-aloud what elements to consider as they examine the visuals. Invite the students to share their thoughts in a class discussion.

### Grade Levels/Standards Addressed

Grades 3–5 (Standard 9.1)
Grades 6–8 (Standard 9.1)

### Activity

Select a portion of the textbook that includes colorful/informative visuals that are appropriate for examination. As students study the pictures closely, have them consider the following questions:

- What does the visual depict? Is it important information?

- Which details does the visual reveal?

Next, assign the reading task. As students read, they should consider how the visual helps them understand the reading better. Ask students to determine if the visual depicts key concepts, helps them find the main idea, highlights important details, introduces additional/new information, or expands their understanding of the information in the text. Remind them to pay close attention to any captions included with the visuals. Have students report their findings during a whole-class discussion. Record their observations on the board or on a transparency. Using the explanations of the visuals, create a summary of the reading.

### Differentiation

ELLs and students reading below grade level will benefit from paired reading and small-group discussion prior to a whole-class discussion. This will provide them with adequate time to prepare and lower their anxiety. Gifted students should be encouraged to find any additional visuals that could accompany the reading selection.

# Using Text Structure and Text Features in Mathematics

## Strategic Planning

Teaching students to read strategically involves instructing them to examine how the important information and ideas are organized in their mathematics textbook and in everything they read. Skilled readers automatically search for the underlying structure of a text to identify how the relationships of the ideas are hierarchically arranged and can readily differentiate important ideas from less important ideas in the selection (Vacca and Vacca 2005).

## Text Sructure

There are different elements to text structure worthy of examination in the mathematics classroom. These approaches range from highlighting external text features (i.e., illustrations, chapter headings, indexes, etc.) to identifying sentence and paragraph organizational patterns (i.e., comparison/contrast, description, etc.) to visually representing the organization of the ideas in the text through graphic organizers (i.e., Venn Diagrams, concept maps, etc.). In general, reading research suggests that almost any approach to teaching the structure of informational texts improves the comprehension and recall of key text information in readers (Duke and Pearson 2002).

The direct instruction of text structure is intended to assist students to anticipate, monitor, and comprehend what they are reading. Looking for and using text structures helps students study texts in order to make connections and think more deeply about the ideas they encounter while reading. If students know what to expect in a mathematics textbook, they spend more time thinking about the content and less time thinking about how it is put together. In addition, students who are familiar and comfortable with a wide variety of text structures can read with greater fluency and can choose to write in the structure that best suits their needs.

## Text Frames

Authors and publishers put forth great effort to design textbooks and informational texts to help readers locate the specific section of the text with the answers to the questions they have. The more students understand the formats of textbooks and informational books, the better equipped they are to remember what they have read, construct meaning about the information, develop new understandings, and apply the ideas they have encountered to different situations.

Teachers should attend to text structures the first time they introduce textbooks and other informational books in their classrooms. Teachers can focus the students' attention on the text features as they preview and skim through their books. Furthermore, teachers should periodically point out how text features affect understanding and highlight various organizational patterns throughout the school term in order to reinforce strategy instruction.

# Using Text Structure and Text Features in Mathematics *(cont.)*

## External and Internal Text Structure

Textbooks include both external and internal text structures. Reading comprehension strategy instruction should assist students in identifying and utilizing both external and internal structures.

## External Text Structure

Informational texts contain format features that serve as the organizational aids that help the reader find information. Most texts include a title page, credits page, table of contents, preface, glossary, index, chapters, visuals, titles, headings, subheadings, etc. Examining external structures is a valuable strategy if it is acknowledged and utilized. For example, students who look at the headings carefully will notice that they guide the reader by highlighting key concepts and ideas.

To the right are the vocabulary terms students should know to discuss and work with external text features. When teachers discuss text features with students, it is important to be precise and consistent in the use of text terms.

## Text Terms

| | |
|---|---|
| appendix | map |
| boldfaced type | margin |
| caption | page |
| chapter | paragraph |
| chart | passage |
| citation | photograph |
| column | picture |
| conclusion | publisher |
| credits page | quotation |
| diagram | references |
| drawing | section |
| excerpt | sketch |
| font size | subheading |
| glossary | subtitle |
| graph | table |
| heading | table of contents |
| illustration | title |
| indenting | title page |
| index | visual aid |
| introduction | year of publication |
| italicized type | |

# Using Text Structure and
# Text Features in Mathematics *(cont.)*

## Internal Text Structure

The internal text structure refers to how the words and paragraphs are logically put together. The purpose of informational text is to *tell, show, describe*, or *explain* (Vacca and Vacca 2005). For the reader to comprehend new information easily, the information must be presented through the logical connections that exist between ideas. Text patterns have emerged in informational texts to aid in the expression of these logical connections. According to Vacca and Vacca (2005), there are five patterns of text that dominate informational writing: *description, sequence, compare and contrast, cause and effect*, and *problem and solution*.

> **Description**—The information about a topic (object, person, animal, idea, event) includes facts, characteristics, traits, and features.
>
> > *Example:* description of whole numbers, real numbers, rational numbers, and integers

> **Sequence**—The facts, events, or concepts are presented in sequential order. The topic is developed in order of importance, or the sequence or steps in a process are given.
>
> > *Example:* how to solve a word problem

> **Compare and Contrast**—The similarities (comparison) and differences (contrast) among facts, people, events, and concepts are presented.
>
> > *Example:* A sphere has a circular shape, but a circle is a plane shape and a sphere is a three-dimensional shape.

> **Cause and Effect**—The information is presented to make clear that certain things (effects) happen as a result of other things (causes).
>
> > *Example:* As you increase the value of a slope, the line becomes steeper.

> **Problem and Solution**—The development of a problem and possible solutions to it are presented.
>
> > *Example:* A domain is a set of possible solutions for a given equation.

# Using Text Structure and
# Text Features in Mathematics *(cont.)*

## Words Specific to Text Structures

As text patterns help authors to disseminate their important information, certain words also help authors on the sentence level. Teachers and students can learn and use the words that signal specific text structures to help them anticipate and understand what they are reading.

| | |
|---|---|
| **Description** | for instance, to begin with, also, in fact, for example, in addition, characteristics of, above, as in, such as, appears to be, between, looks like, outside, under, across, behind, down, near, over, along, below, in back of, on top of, beside, in front of, onto, to the right/left |
| **Sequence** | on (date), not long after, now, as, before, after, afterward, as soon as, when, first, second, third, next, then, last, finally, end, middle, beginning, during, initially, immediately, preceding, not long after, today, soon, until, following, meanwhile, when |
| **Compare and Contrast** | although, as well as, as opposed to, both, but, compared with, different from, either...or, neither...nor, even though, however, instead of, in common, on the other hand, otherwise, similar to, similarly, still, yet |
| **Cause and Effect and Problem and Solution** | accordingly, as a result of, because, begins with, consequently, effects of, finally, first, for this reason, how to, how, if...then, in order to, is caused by, leads/led to, may be due to, nevertheless, next, since, so that, steps involved, subsequently, therefore, this led to, thus, when...then |

# Strategies for Attending to Text Structure in Mathematics

## Textbook Scavenger Hunt

### Background Information

A fun way for students to familiarize themselves with the features of their textbooks is to have them complete a scavenger hunt (Robb 2003). Students can complete the activity all at once or it can be organized for students to complete over a number of days. Students can complete the activity with a partner or in small groups.

### Grade Levels/Standards Addressed

Grades 1–2 (Standard 7.1)
Grades 3–5 (Standard 7.4)

### Activity

Activate students' prior knowledge about text features through whole-class questioning. Review the different features of a textbook with the class while skimming through a book. Divide the class into groups of four students. Distribute copies of the Textbook Scavenger Hunt handout (page 184). Instruct the students to work together to complete the handout. As students work on the handout, circle the room to provide assistance as necessary. When they have completed the handout, call on the different teams to share their findings. Write their findings on the board and discuss them further.

### Differentiation

ELLs should have a vocabulary list of text terms with definitions available to them during the activity. Provide them with extra time to complete the task or have some of the questions answered for them. Students reading below grade level should approach the questions in the order they find most comfortable and should not be rushed to complete the task. Gifted students should compete to see who finishes the task first.

**Name:** _____

# Textbook Scavenger Hunt

**Directions:** Work with your team member(s) and use the textbook to complete the following questions.

1. **Index**    number of pages _____ location _____

   Locate and write a key topic that has several pages of information.

   _____

   Find a topic that has a single page listed.

   _____

2. **Table of Contents**    number of pages _____ location _____ number of sections _____

   List three sections that interest you.

   _____

3. **Glossary**    number of pages _____ location _____

   What kind of information does it contain?  How can a glossary help you?

   _____

4. **Chapters**

   Look at the first page of a chapter.  List the information here.

   _____

   Look at the last page of a chapter.  What do you find there?  How can this help you?

   _____

5. **Boldfaced Words**    List three boldfaced words in the same chapter.  What do they mean?

   In what ways can you use a textbook to find the meanings of words?

   _____

6. **Photographs**    page number _____ description _____

   Study the picture and the caption and write down what you learned.

   _____

7. **Visual Aids**    page number _____ description _____

   Locate a graph, chart, diagram, or map.  Study it and read all of the print that accompanies it.
   Explain what this visual aid can teach you.

   _____

8. **Other**    page number _____ description _____

   What other features are in your textbook?  How do these help you learn new information?

   _____

# Strategies for Attending to Text Structure in Mathematics *(cont.)*

## Table of Contents Predictions

### Background Information

One way to highlight text structure for students is to combine it with another reading comprehension strategy, such as predicting. Developing predicting skills in students helps them set their purposes for reading, increases their motivation to read, instills curiosity, and heightens their motivation to learn (Ryder and Graves 2003). Students can use the table of contents prior to beginning a new section of the text to predict what they think they will be reading about. Allowing students to predict the contents of the reading enables students to establish what they expect to find in the reading, which motivates them. When they read the section, they check to determine whether or not their predictions were correct. In addition, the teacher is able to remind students how to use text structure to locate and summarize information.

### Grade Levels/Standards Addressed

Grades 1–2 (Standard 7.1)
Grades 3–5 (Standard 7.4)

### Activity

Before beginning a new unit or chapter of the textbook, ask students to open their books and examine the table of contents for the new section. Have them write down what they expect to read about and hope to learn when they read the chapter. Place students in small groups and ask them to share their expectations with one another.

Encourage them to discuss their ideas. Instruct them to make a list of things they expect to read and learn. Conduct a whole-class discussion in which you compile a list of what the students expect to learn on chart paper. Place the paper on a bulletin board, and as you progress through the reading, check off the concepts and ideas that students learn from the reading. When the students have finished the chapter, review the list to determine how accurate their predictions were, to identify what items they expected to learn about but did not, and to make a new list of things they learned that they did not anticipate learning. Remind students that the table of contents is a tool for locating information, but it also contains main ideas and key concepts that will be included in the reading.

### Differentiation

It is important to assess the prior knowledge of ELLs on the topic before beginning this activity. Build on their prior knowledge if necessary to make the activity useful and relevant to them. Students reading below grade level may need the teacher to read some of the chapter aloud or do a paired reading. Encourage gifted students to independently explore the topics not covered in the textbook that the class predicted.

# Strategies for Attending to
# Text Structure in Mathematics *(cont.)*

## Creating Captions

## Background Information

An important component of textbooks and other informational texts is the use of visual images and the print associated with them. Students may look closely at the images when directed to do so by the teacher, but they often gloss over the titles and captions. These captions highlight important information from the reading. Sometimes the captions include additional information that is not included in the reading. Students can synthesize their new knowledge by combining summarizing and visual representation strategies in the Creating Captions activity (Hoyt 2002). Teachers provide students with visual images (pictures, photographs, sketches, illustrations, and diagrams) and ask the students to write an appropriate caption for the image. To do so, the students must identify the main idea and highlight its importance in a succinct manner.

## Grade Levels/Standards Addressed

Grades 1–2 (Standard 7.3)
Grades 3–5 (Standard 7.5)
Grades 6–8 (Standard 7.3)

## Activity

Introduce the importance of the captions that accompany visuals in textbooks and informational texts. Have students look through their textbooks to examine how the captions relate key concepts from the reading. After students have completed reading a selection, gather together a number of visuals that could accompany the reading.

Delete any titles or captions. Model how to construct a caption with one of the visuals (be brief; highlight important information). Encourage students to ask questions. Introduce another visual and ask the students to create the caption as a whole class. Discuss the process again. Next, place the students in small groups. Distribute sticky notes to each group. Distribute copies of the same visuals to each group, and instruct students to use the reading to create an appropriate caption for the visual using the sticky note. As students present their captions for the visual to the class, write them down on the board. When students are finished presenting, work together as a class to revise the captions into one that synthesizes all of the information from their captions.

## Differentiation

During the modeling stage, be sure to repeat and rephrase your explanations to help ELLs understand. Students reading below grade level may struggle to write a caption, so it may help to have them underline important words in the reading prior to beginning the caption writing. Gifted students should be encouraged to use literary devices to make their captions particularly catchy and interesting.

# Strategies for Attending to Text Structure in Mathematics *(cont.)*

## Flag Words

### Background Information

Writers have adopted the use of specific words to indicate to the reader that they will be using a specific text pattern to convey their ideas. Readers' fluency with text depends on the ability to anticipate what information is going to be revealed and how it is going to be revealed based on the words used in a passage. Flag Words (Lenski, Wham, and Johns 1999) is an activity that helps students identify specific text patterns so that they can better understand what they will be reading. Teaching students specific flag words that signal common textual patterns enhances the students' ability to use the organization of the text to better comprehend the content.

### Grade Levels/Standards Addressed

Grades 3–5 (Standard 7.7)
Grades 6–8 (Standard 7.1)

### Activity

Prepare for the activity by selecting a section of the text and identifying the main organizational pattern used. Be sure to select a section that contains an easily identifiable pattern. Prepare a list of common Flag Words for this text structure appropriate for the grade level (see page 182 for common words for grades 1–8). Provide the students with photocopies of the reading selection, or give them sticky notes so that they can make notes. Explain that authors use Flag Words to provide readers with specific clues to help them understand how the text will be organized and what information is most important. Use examples from the mathematics textbook to model the strategy for students. Model how to identify the Flag Words in the reading and then demonstrate how to annotate the text to highlight important ideas and information. Distribute the photocopies and highlighter pens or sticky notes and provide ample time for the students to read the text and make notations. When the students are finished, ask them to share the Flag Words they located and what they wrote in the margins. Be sure to discuss how this strategy helps students understand what they are reading. Point out that it also helps them use different text structures when they are writing.

### Differentiation

ELLs and students reading below grade level may prefer to complete this activity with a partner. Gifted students should be encouraged to work independently and may need little direct instruction.

# Strategies for Attending to Text Structure in Mathematics *(cont.)*

## Graphic Organizers

### Background Information

As the Report of the National Reading Panel (2000) points out, a graph is a visual depiction of relationships. Teachers ask students to organize the ideas in a mathematics text to show the relationships based on what they have read. Thus, the term *graphic organizer* is a visual depiction of how ideas in a mathematics text are interrelated, connected, and organized. Graphic organizers are a visual form of traditional outlining. However, they are more flexible and stimulating for students to use because of their visual nature. Graphic organizers require the students to process information that they have read and have seen, which enhances their retention and recall. Using graphic organizers helps readers remember what they read and improves reading comprehension and achievement (Trabasso and Bouchard 2002). There are hundreds of graphic organizers available to teachers. The examples for this activity are specific to teaching students the components of different text structures.

### Grade Levels/Standards Addressed

Grades 1–2 (Standard 7.3)
Grades 3–5 (Standard 7.3)
Grades 6–8 (Standard 7.3)

### Activity

Begin by explaining that when readers understand how a book is organized, they are better able to organize new information and understand it. Explain that graphic organizers help students organize and remember what they have read. Select a passage from any mathematics informational book or the textbook for the students to read. Prepare the students for the activity by explaining that you will model how to use a graphic organizer to help

them understand how the information is organized to improve comprehension and memory. Instruct the students in the internal text patterns found in the selected text (see page 181). Explain in great detail the components of the text structure as you write them on the board. For example, if you are explaining *sequence* to students, show specific examples of ordered things or events. Solving a linear equation would be a great example to use to illustrate this concept. If a linear equation is not solved in a specific order of steps, it is difficult to come up with the correct answer. Model how to use the graphic organizer by displaying it on the board or on a transparency and distribute individual copies to the students. Explain how to read the text and identify the important information to include in the graphic organizer. Using the example above, you might point out the important information regarding ordered steps in problem solving and solving linear equations, and then demonstrate how to best include it in the graphic organizer. As you read the passage aloud, pause and do a think-aloud to show the students exactly how to identify the important information from the text. Ask them to read the rest of the passage and add more information to their graphic organizers. Invite the students to discuss their graphic organizers to clarify and expand on their information.

### Differentiation

Teachers can scaffold the information to be placed in the graphic organizers for ELLs and students reading below grade level to lower their anxiety. Both groups of students may benefit from working in pairs or small groups to complete the graphic organizer. Gifted students may require little or no instruction and may be given an alternative assignment if warranted.

# Strategies for Attending to Text Structure in Mathematics (cont.)

## Graphic Organizers (cont.)

**Sequence**

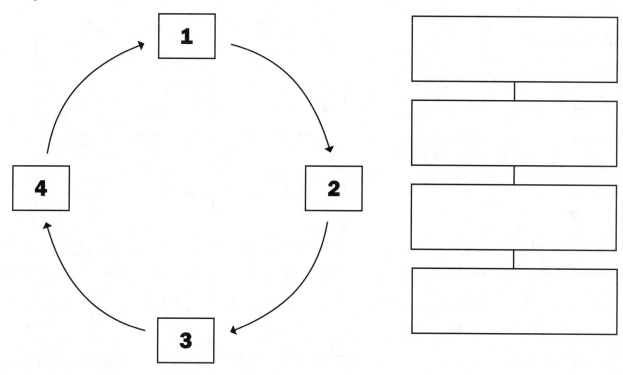

**Compare and Contrast**

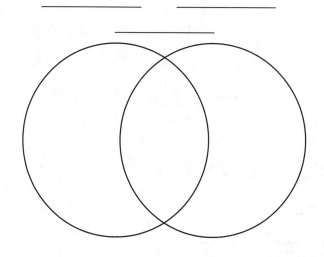

| | Name 1 | Name 2 |
|---|---|---|
| **Attribute 1** | | |
| **Attribute 2** | | |
| **Attribute 3** | | |

# Strategies for Attending to
# Text Structure in Mathematics (cont.)

## Graphic Organizers (cont.)

**Cause and Effect**

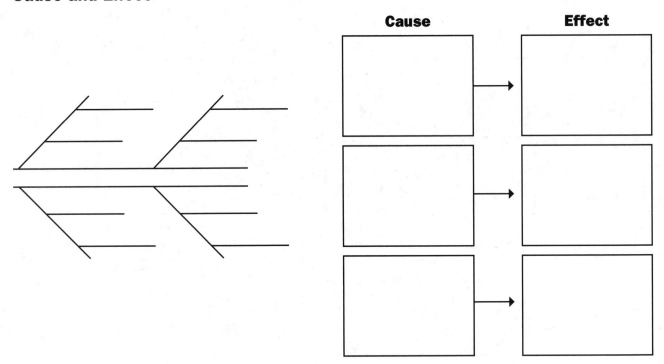

Cause        Effect

**Problem and Solution**

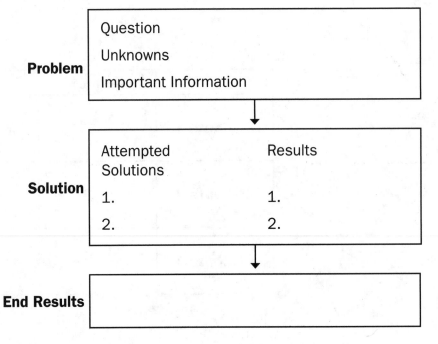

## Graphic Organizers (cont.)

**Description**

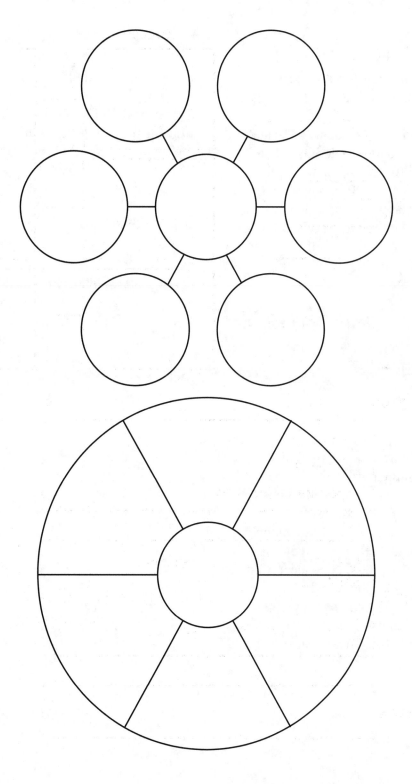

# Strategies for Attending to Text Structure in Mathematics *(cont.)*

## Constructing Informational Texts

### Background Information

Hoyt (2002) suggests that mathematics teachers can help students learn more about text features by creating a big book on a mathematics topic as a class or allowing individual students to create small books on a mathematics topic independently. The students can construct the book and dedicate one page to each text feature. By applying their knowledge and understanding of text features, students can improve their retention of the information over the long term as well as utilize the elements of text features in their own writing.

### Grade Levels/Standards Addressed

Grades 1–2 (Standard 7.3)
Grades 3–5 (Standard 7.3)

### Activity

After students have studied the different text features appropriate to their grade level, inform them that they will be creating a big class book on a mathematics topic they have just finished studying. Use an informational text as a model to review the different text features and discuss their characteristics. As a class, generate a list of text features that the book should highlight (see page 180 for possible text features to highlight). Allow the students to determine how many pages of the book should be devoted to each text feature.

Either place the students in pairs to complete their pages or allow them to work independently on their pages. Before the book is complete, have the students present drafts of their pages to the class for review and approval. When the book is complete, bind it and send it to another class to share with other students.

### Differentiation

ELLs may prefer to select text features for their pages that are visual in nature. Students reading below grade level may need additional modeling and support as they construct their pages. Gifted students may prefer to work independently and might enjoy making the bookbinding, which can include a title and summary of the class for the back cover.

# Strategies for Attending to Text Structure in Mathematics *(cont.)*

## Constructing Informational Texts *(cont.)*

**Grades 1–2 Example**

| Page Number | Topic | Text Feature Highlighted |
|---|---|---|
| 1 | Money | table of contents |
| 2 | Dollar bill | illustration |
| 3 | Penny, nickel, dime, quarter | boldfaced type |
| 4 | Child buying a toy | diagram with caption |
| 5 | Denominators | chart with names of each and value |
| 6 | | glossary |
| 7 | | index |

**Grades 3–5 Example**

| Page Number | Topic | Text Feature Highlighted |
|---|---|---|
| Cover/Back | Perimeter | visuals, title, summary |
| 1 | Perimeter | table of contents |
| 2 | Circles | illustrations with captions |
| 3 | Squares | chart with stats |
| 4 | Rectangles | illustration with caption |
| 5 | Triangles | diagram with labels |
| 6 | Diamonds | boldfaced type and illustration |
| 7 | Pentagons | title and subtitle |
| 8 | Hexagons | diagram with labels |
| 9 | Octagons | photos with captions |
| 10 | Nonagons | chart with stats |
| 11 | | glossary |
| 12 | | index |

# Multiple Reading Comprehension Strategy Instruction

## What Is Multiple Strategy Instruction?

While many researchers have focused on how the explicit instruction of individual reading strategies enhances students' ability to comprehend textual materials, combining reading strategies in a multiple strategy approach has proven to be very effective. The National Reading Panel Report (2000) makes it clear that the multiple strategies approach to reading comprehension is highly effective in assisting students in becoming more efficient and effective readers.

The multiple strategy approach in reading comprehension has been given a number of names by researchers: comprehension routines (Duke and Pearson 2002); process-based comprehension instruction (Block, Schaller, Joy, and Gaine 2002); multiple strategy intervention (Baker 2002); and comprehensive approach to comprehension instruction (Pearson and Duke 2002). A rose is a rose, no matter what the name. The National Reading Panel Report (2000) reviewed 38 multiple strategy studies—more significant studies were conducted in the area of the multiple strategy approach to improving reading comprehension in the classroom than any other topic. As the Report states, "The multiple strategy instruction model represents an evolution in the field from the study of individual strategies to their flexible and multiple use" (4–46). The research reviewed provides considerable scientific support for the use of multiple strategies when instructing in reading comprehension.

## Why Does Combining Strategies Work?

Reading is a cognitive task that requires readers to coordinate multiple skills simultaneously. Skilled reading involves an ongoing adaptation of multiple cognitive processes (The National Reading Panel Report 2000). When students are instructed to use reading comprehension strategies in combination, they learn how to think in terms of the two strategies simultaneously. As a result, they develop greater flexibility and coordination to better understand what they are reading. If one strategy does not work effectively, students will still comprehend the text because the other strategy has been utilized. This approach to reading comprehension teaches students how to relate multiple strategies at specific points in the text when needed (Block, Schaller, Joy, and Gaine 2002). Because students are made aware that the reading strategies do not have to work in isolation, they indirectly learn to select which strategies will work best for different reading situations. As a result, considerable success has been achieved in improving text comprehension by instructing students how to use more than one strategy during the course of reading (The National Reading Panel Report 2000).

# Multiple Reading Comprehension Strategy Instruction *(cont.)*

## Teaching How to Interrelate Comprehension Strategies

The multiple strategies approach described later in this chapter explains teaching approaches that have been tested and proven effective in the classroom. Teachers, however, can combine reading comprehension strategies in their instruction on their own. The National Reading Panel Report (2000) suggests that this technique best serves students in grades 3–8. In this approach, teachers can choose to teach the following (Block, Schaller, Joy, and Gaine 2002):

- How to add depth and breadth to knowledge through intertextuality, summarizing, inferring, imaging, interpreting the author's intentions, reflecting, paraphrasing, identifying the gist, organizing, predicting, making connections among words, facts, concepts, and the historical and political context in which they are written and read.

- How to simultaneously comprehend literally, inferentially, and applicably by establishing different purposes for reading.

- How to think metacognitively and to clarify by using fix-up strategies and continuous self-monitoring.

- How to fill in the gaps in both narrative and expository texts by processing the text continuously while reading.

# Approaches to Multiple Reading Comprehension Strategy Instruction

## Reciprocal Teaching

Four comprehension strategies—predicting, questioning, clarifying, and summarizing—are combined in Reciprocal Teaching. Reciprocal Teaching (Palinscar 1982, as cited by Duke and Pearson 2002) utilizes the gradual release of responsibility from the teacher to the student in each part of the process. In the first stage of the process, the teacher models different reading strategies, explains exactly what the strategies are, and explains exactly how they are used. The teacher selects two or more combinations of four strategies: question generation, summarization, clarification, and prediction, and uses direct instruction with the students. Initially, the teacher guides the readers as they apply and practice the strategies together while reading a selection of the text. The teacher models how to use the strategies by providing examples and conducting think-alouds during the reading to demonstrate how to use the strategies in conjunction with one another. After much practice, the students can work in small groups. When the students demonstrate proficiency in using the strategies within small groups, the teacher gradually releases the responsibility of utilizing the reading strategies to the individual students to use independently.

Duke and Pearson (2002) describe a typical Reciprocal Teaching session as such:

> The session usually begins with a review of the main points from the previous day's reading, or the students may make predictions about the upcoming reading based on the title and pictures. Next, all students read the first paragraph of the text silently to themselves.

A student assigned to act as teacher asks a question about the paragraph, summarizes the paragraph, asks for clarification if needed, and predicts what might be in the next paragraph. During the process, the teacher prompts the student-teacher as needed and in the end provides feedback about the student-teacher's work.

Reciprocal Teaching sessions usually last 20–40 minutes, and more than one student can take the role of the teacher during the session. The teacher's role is to guide the students through modeling and scaffolding. Throughout the session, the teacher regularly reminds the students of why learning the reading comprehension strategies is important and how it will improve their skills.

Reading researchers have reviewed a number of studies of Reciprocal Teaching and have concluded that it is effective at improving comprehension of text (Duke and Pearson 2002). Dramatic improvements in reading comprehension skills are evident after about 20 sessions of properly conducted Reciprocal Teaching (Snowball, n.d.).

# Approaches to Multiple Reading Comprehension Strategy Instruction (cont.)

## Concept-Oriented Reading Instruction

One approach to reading instruction that can be specific to mathematics is Concept-Oriented Reading Instruction (CORI) (Guthrie, Bennett, and McGough 1994). The researchers developed the framework in response to the problem of illiteracy among students, who choose not to read frequently or broadly, despite their reading abilities. CORI was developed with the purpose of increasing the students' engagement in reading and is designed to help students learn about a variety of subjects while exploring and reading nonfiction books. The students select a topic of study, read about it from a wide variety of resources, and determine the important concepts and critical details related to the topic. The students also evaluate and compare the texts used and produce an artifact that demonstrates the synthesis of information learned.

The framework involves students engaging in the following (Guthrie, Bennett, and McGough 1994):

- Observing and personalizing "real-world" problems as a basis for intrinsic motivations for reading
- Learning a variety of cognitive strategies for exploring these problems (including reading comprehension strategies)
- Interacting socially to construct conceptual knowledge
- Communicating their understanding to genuine audiences

There are five "instructional dimensions" involved in CORI: observing and personalizing, searching and retrieving, comprehending and integrating, communicating to others, and peer-to-peer interaction. Each dimension can be adapted to involve the direct instruction of reading comprehension strategies that include activating and building on prior knowledge, imaging, text feature analysis, and summarizing. Because CORI, unlike other multiple strategy approaches, involves wide reading to increase motivation to read for pleasure, it is worthy of practice.

### Observing and Personalizing

In this phase, teachers instruct students to observe and think about the concrete objects and events in the real world around them to motivate the students to engage in the reading. Students select a topic (and subtopics) of inquiry based on their personal interests (a part of their prior experiences) to help them explore the world around them. At this time, teachers can engage in activating and building on prior knowledge.

### Searching and Retrieving

In this phase, students are taught how to locate the materials related to their general interests. Students use mathematics books to learn more about the subtopics they select. The teacher guides students to use text structure and feature analysis to locate information relevant to the topic from a wide variety of sources (books, pages of an illustrated reference work, articles, tables, charts). Students are taught how to skim and scrutinize the materials they select and how to scan texts, graphs, charts, maps, and tables for important information. These tasks involve the direct instruction of the analysis of text features.

# Approaches to Multiple Reading Comprehension Strategy Instruction *(cont.)*

## Concept–Oriented Reading Instruction *(cont.)*

### Comprehending and Integrating

In this phase, teachers use direct instruction to teach students how to determine the main idea of a reading selection, detect crucial details, summarize what they have read, make comparisons between the texts, develop criteria for evaluating a book, and critically reflect on the author's point of view and presentation of the information. Students are taught summarizing skills and questioning skills during this phase so that they can better integrate their new knowledge into their conceptual understanding.

### Communicating to Others

In this phase, the students are directed to construct a tangible artifact that synthesizes what they have learned and represents a coherent message. Students are taught how to identify important information, organize the information in a coherent form, and express their ideas precisely and convincingly to an audience. Teachers instruct students in using text features, visualization, and summarizing for presentation purposes.

### Peer-to-Peer Interaction

An integral part of the CORI framework is the creation of a learning community through peer-to-peer interactions. This community works together to sustain interest in learning, permits higher-order thinking and integration of ideas, and enables the students to use social processes to aid in their construction of meaning. The students engage in peer-led discussions with the common goal of understanding the reading comprehension strategies that are the focus of the lessons.

### Why It Works

The research on CORI demonstrates that students read a greater number of texts and a wider variety of texts within the CORI instructional framework (Guthrie, Bennett, and McGough 1994). Furthermore, students are more motivated to read because the reading comprehension strategies are taught and practiced within a rich conceptual context. As the authors state, "When a strategy is taught in an intrinsically interesting, conceptually compelling context, students are motivated to learn it. The strategy is useful because it serves students' immediate and larger interests, and reading is not merely a cognitive exercise" (Guthrie, Bennett, and McGough 1994, 18).

# Approaches to Multiple Reading Comprehension Strategy Instruction *(cont.)*

## Students Achieving Independent Learning

The reading comprehension strategies emphasized in Students Achieving Independent Learning (SAIL) are predicting, visualizing, questioning, clarifying, making associations (connecting prior knowledge to text), and summarizing. As in Reciprocal Teaching, the teacher instructs students in how to use these strategies through explicit instruction and think-alouds. However, the focus is to help students learn how to choose the most effective strategies to use for any given text. Therefore, students focus on interpreting the text as they practice the reading comprehension strategies with a variety of texts. When using the SAIL routine, students are encouraged to articulate what the strategies are and how to use them, so they are working on developing their metacognitive skills. Furthermore, the routine enables the students to discuss with each other the advantages and disadvantages of each strategy in different situations, so the students learn to determine when it is most appropriate to use a particular strategy and why.

When using the SAIL routine in the classroom, there is no particular order in which to teach the strategies. Because strategy use really depends on the given situation, the students should learn when it is best to use a particular strategy. The teacher provides a wide variety of texts to work with and models what thinking processes work best for different texts. The students learn how to apply multiple strategies as needed. Also, there is a greater focus on the student's interpretation of the text rather than "the right answers" (Duke and Pearson 2002). SAIL requires many small-group and whole-class discussions so that the students can talk to one another about the reading. They should also practice their own think-aloud skills as they read independently and share their thinking with each other.

Duke and Pearson (2002) summarize the qualitative research on SAIL by stating that it provides students with rich, motivating interactions with reading materials. Furthermore, with SAIL, the students become more sophisticated at using reading comprehension strategies over time. In addition, students in classrooms that use SAIL outperform the students in non-SAIL classrooms in standardized reading comprehension and vocabulary tests, and they also have better recall of the content in the reading.

# Approaches to Multiple Reading Comprehension Strategy Instruction *(cont.)*

## Collaborative Strategic Reading

Collaborative Strategic Reading (CSR) (Klingner and Vaughn 2002) combines both reading comprehension strategy instruction and cooperative learning strategies that many teachers already comfortably employ in their classrooms. CSR has been successful in improving comprehension in learning disabled students and students learning English due to peer interaction.

In CSR, teachers place students in small, mixed-ability, cooperative groups to work together as they apply four reading strategies to their text. The framework utilizes prior knowledge, prediction, monitoring comprehension, summarizing, and generating questions in the four stages of reading called preview, click and clunk, get the gist, and wrap-up.

The teacher begins by introducing CSR to the whole class and models the entire CSR framework to help the students understand the plan. The teacher provides explicit instruction for using each of the reading strategies in the subsequent days. Using think-alouds, the teacher models how to verbalize thinking as he or she applies each of the strategies while reading a section of text. The teacher increases student involvement as they become more proficient at using the strategies and gradually releases responsibility to them.

### Preview

Prior to reading a selection, the teacher models how to activate prior knowledge before reading so that students can make accurate predictions about the content of the reading. In doing so, the teacher helps generate interest in the topic. Teachers instruct students to spend approximately eight minutes to determine what the passage is about, who is described in the text, when the passage takes place, and where the text describes information that they already know about the topic. The students learn how to use the following to help them in previewing: headings and subheadings; words that are italicized, bolded, or underlined; pictures, tables, and graphs; and questions or key information highlighted in the columns or sidebars.

### Click and Clunk

This strategy teaches students to monitor comprehension during reading by identifying difficult words and concepts in the passage and using fix-up strategies when the text does not make sense. Students "click" it when they recognize information in the reading and know it well, and they "clunk" it when they encounter information they do not understand or need to know more about. Teachers instruct students in how to monitor their reading comprehension by recording clunks to discuss with their peers and the teacher. They "declunk" words by applying the fix-up strategies they learn from clunk cards that instruct them to reread the sentence with the clunk, reread the sentences before and after the clunk, look for prefixes or suffixes in the word, and break the word down to find smaller, recognizable words.

## Collaborative Strategic Reading *(cont.)*

### Get the Gist

By "getting the gist," students learn how to restate the main ideas or the most critical information in the text during reading. They are taught how to identify the most important points and retell what they have read in their own words. To teach students how to summarize effectively, they are instructed to get the gist in as few words as possible (ten words) and exclude unnecessary details while conveying the most meaning. Students should interact to review what aspects of their gist should be kept or dropped.

### Wrap-up

When students "wrap-up" the reading, they summarize what has been learned from the reading and generate possible teacher-generated questions. They also answer the questions they have formulated as this helps them review the important information. In doing so, students improve their comprehension of the content and their recall of the information. Teachers can instruct students to use question stems to help them formulate literal and higher-order thinking questions on index cards.

### CSR Materials

**Cue cards**—The teacher can generate cue cards for each of the members of the cooperative groups with instructions for the different roles that students can take. These cards help students stay focused on the task. For example, during the preview, a cue card might read, "Let's brainstorm and write everything we know about the topic in our learning logs."

**Learning logs**—Learning logs can take many forms, but all help students record their ideas and facilitate cooperative learning. The learning log should ask the students to identify what they already know about the topic, what they predict they will learn, questions they have about the important ideas in the passage, and the gist of the reading. Students should write down the clunks they encounter as well.

# Approaches to Multiple Reading Comprehension Strategy Instruction (cont.)

## Question Answer Relationships

Question Answer Relationships (QAR) (Raphael and Au 2005) is a multiple strategy approach that gives students and teachers a common language about prior knowledge and questioning strategies. The creators argue that students and teachers need to use a common language about reading so that they can more easily discuss the processes involved in listening and reading comprehension during think-alouds and modeling. The QAR strategy allows students to categorize types of questions easily, which enables them to more readily answer them.

The first step in beginning QAR with students is to introduce them to the common language. Students learn that they use either prior knowledge (In My Head) or information gained from the book (In the Book) to generate and answer questions. Teachers use explicit instruction to teach students In the Book strategies, such as how to skim or scan the text for information, reread, or use clues from the title of the reading or from chapter headings to locate or recall relevant information. The teacher can begin by introducing a text and asking students to generate questions based on the title, pictures, and other text features prior to reading and to record the information on sticky notes. The teacher then asks them to consider whether the information is located In My Head or In the Book and records the information on a large wall chart to make the distinction clear to the students.

As students gain greater skill at using QAR, the teacher can build on their understanding of the strategies involved in the framework. Once students are confident in using In the Book, the teacher can introduce Right There and Think and Search. And, once the students show proficiency at using In My Head, the teacher can introduce Author and Me and On My Own.

### Right There Questions

The answers to Right There questions are located directly in the reading materials. They are the literal level of questions that ask *who, what, where, why, when, how*, etc. These questions sometimes begin with "According to the passage…" or include the aforementioned journalistic words.

### Think and Search Questions

Thinking and searching requires the students to think about what they have read and make connections in order to relate the information and ideas in a passage to each other. The students must look back at the reading selection, try to find the information needed to answer the question, and then think about how the information or ideas fit together. These questions sometimes include the phrases, "compare and contrast…," "the main idea of the passage…," and "what caused…".

## Question Answer Relationships *(cont.)*

### Author and Me Questions

These questions require the students to use ideas and information that is not directly stated in the reading selection to find the answers. The students must think about what they have read to formulate their own opinions. These questions are inferential and sometimes begin with "The author implies…," "The passage suggests…," and "The speaker's attitude…".

### On My Own Questions

Students can answer On My Own questions using their prior knowledge and experiences. These questions usually do not appear on tests because they do not refer to the reading passage. On My Own questions usually include the phrases "In your opinion…" or "Based on your experience…".

When teaching students how to correctly identify the four different types of questions, teachers should begin with whole-class instruction. The teacher can use a read aloud and ask the students to pose questions about the reading after they have completed the passage. The teacher can write their questions on sticky notes and then place them in the appropriate categories on a large chart paper. To further their understanding of the different types of questions, the teacher can prepare a number of questions about the reading passage and ask them to place the questions in the correct category. Gradually, the teacher releases the responsibility to the students as they work in small groups to label the different question-answer relationships. Eventually, the teacher can give the students a reading selection to complete in pairs and require the pairs to generate a given number of questions for each question-answer relationship.

QAR is an effective approach to teaching reading comprehension strategies because it emphasizes the value of scanning, skimming, and rereading to locate information as well as differentiating new knowledge from prior experiences.

# Works Cited

Baker, L. 2002. Metacognition in comprehension instruction. In *Comprehension instruction: Research-based best practices*, ed. C. C. Block and M. Pressley, 77–95. New York: The Guilford Press.

Beck, I. L., M. G. McKeown, R. Hamilton, and L. Kucan. 1997. *Questioning the author: An approach for enhancing student engagement with text.* Newark, DE: International Reading Association.

Blachowicz, C. L. Z. and P. Fisher. 2000. Vocabulary instruction. In vol. 3 of *Handbook of reading research*, ed. R. Barr, M. L. Kamil, P. B. Mosenthal, and P. D. Pearson, 503–524. Mahwah, NJ: Lawrence Earlbaum Associates, Inc.

Block, C. C., and S. E. Israel. 2004. The ABCs of performing highly effective think-alouds. *The Reading Teacher* 58(2): 154–167. Newark, DE: International Reading Association.

Block, C. C., and M. Pressley. 2003. Best practices in comprehension instruction. In *Best practices in literacy instruction.* 2nd ed. Ed. L. M. Morrow, L. B. Gambrell and M. Pressley, 111–126. New York: The Guilford Press.

Block, C. C., J. L. Schaller, J. A. Joy, and P. Gaine. 2002. Process-based comprehension instruction: Perspectives of four reading educators. In *Comprehension instruction: Research-based best practices*, ed. C. C. Block and M. Pressley, 42–61. New York: The Guilford Press.

Christen, W. L., and T. J. Murphy. 1991. Increasing comprehension by activating prior knowledge. ERIC Digest. Bloomington, IN: ERIC Clearinghouse on Reading, English, and Communication.

Clark, K. F., and M. F. Graves. 2005. Scaffolding students' comprehension of text. *The Reading Teacher* 58(6): 570–580.

Cotton, K. 1988. Classroom questioning. Northwest Regional Educational Laboratory. http://www.nwrel.org/scpd/sirs/3/cu5.html.

Dechant, E. 1991. *Understanding and Teaching Reading: An Interactive Model.* Hillsdale, NJ: Lawrence Erlbaum Associates, Inc.

Duke, N. K., and P. D. Pearson. 2002. Effective practices for developing reading comprehension. In *What research has to say about reading instruction.* 3rd ed. Ed. A. E. Farstup and S. J. Samuels, 205–242. Newark, DE: International Reading Association, Inc.

Frayer, D. A., W. D. Frederick, and H. J. Klausmeier. 1969. A schema for testing the level of concept mastery. Working Paper No. 16. Madison: Wisconsin Research and Development Center for Cognitive Learning.

Gambrell, L. B. and P. B. Jawitz. 1993. Mental imagery, text illustrations, and children's story comprehension and recall. *Reading Research Quarterly* 28:264–276.

Gambrell, L. B. and P. S. Koskinen. 2002. Imagery: A strategy for enhancing comprehension. In *Comprehension instruction: Research-based best practices*, ed. C. C. Block and M. Pressley, 305–318. New York: The Guilford Press.

Guthrie, J. T., L. Bennett, and K. McGough. 1994. Concept-oriented reading instruction: An integrated curriculum to develop motivations and strategies for reading. *Reading Research Report No. 10.* University of Georgia and University of Maryland: National Reading Research Center.

# Works Cited (cont.)

Hayes, D. A. 1989. Helping students GRASP the knack of writing summaries. *Journal of Reading* 32:96–101.

Hoyt, L. 2002. *Make it real: Strategies for success with informational texts.* Portsmouth, NH: Heinemann.

Keene, E. O. 2002. From good to memorable: Characteristics of highly effective comprehension teaching. In *Improving Comprehension Instruction*, ed. C. C. Block, L. B. Gambrell, and M. Pressley, 80–105. San Francisco: Jossey-Bass.

Keene, E. O., and S. Zimmerman. 1997. *Mosaic of thought: Teaching comprehension in a reader's workshop.* Portsmouth, NH: Heinemann.

Klingner, J. K., and S. Vaughn. 2002. Promoting reading comprehension, content learning, and English acquisition through collaborative strategic reading. *The Reading Teacher* 52(7): 738–47.

Kragler, S., C. A. Walker, and L. E. Martin. 2005. Strategy instruction in primary content textbooks. *The Reading Teacher* 59(3): 254–261.

Krashen, S. 88 Generalizations about free voluntary reading. http://www.sdkrashen.com/handouts/88Generalizations/index.html

Kujawa, S., and L. Huske. 1995. *The strategic teaching and reading project guidebook.* Rev. ed. Oak Brook, IL: North Central Regional Educational Laboratory.

Lapp, D., J. Flood, and N. Farnan. 1996. *Content reading and learning instructional strategies.* 2nd ed. Boston: Allyn & Bacon.

Lenski, S. D., M. A. Wham, and J. L. Johns. 1999. *Reading and learning strategies for middle and high school students.* Dubuque, IA: Kendall/Hunt Publishing Company.

Moore, D. W., S. A. Moore, P. M. Cunningham, and J. W. Cunningham. 2002. *Developing readers and writers in the content area K-12.* 5th ed. Boston: Allyn & Bacon.

Morrow, L. M. 2003. Motivating lifelong voluntary reading. In *Handbook of research on teaching the English language arts,* ed. J. Flood, D. Lapp, J. R. Squire, and J. M. Jensen, 857–867. Mahwah, NJ: Lawrence Erlbaum Associates, Publishers.

Nagy, W. E. and J. A. Scott. 2000. Vocabulary processes. In vol. 3 of *Handbook of reading research,* ed. M. L. Kamil and R. Barr, 269–284. Mahwah, NJ: Lawrence Earlbaum Associates, Inc.

National Institute of Child Health and Human Development. 2000. *Teaching children to read: An evidence-based assessment of the scientific research literature on reading and its implications for reading instruction.* Report of the National Reading Panel. Washington, DC: U.S. Government Printing Office.

Neufeld, P. 2005. Comprehension instruction in content area classes. *The Reading Teacher* 59(4): 302–312. Newark, DE: International Reading Association, Inc.

Neuman, S. 1988. Enhancing children's comprehension through previewing. In *Dialogues in literacy reseach,* ed. J. Readence and R. S. Baldwin, 219–224. 37th Yearbook of the National Reading Conference. Chicago: National Reading Conference.

# Works Cited (cont.)

Pearson, P. D. and N. K. Duke. 2002. Comprehension instruction in the primary grades. In *Comprehension instruction: Research-based best practices*, ed. C. C. Block and M. Pressley, 247–258. New York: The Guilford Press.

Pressley, M. 2000. What should comprehension instruction be the instruction of? In vol. 3 of *Handbook of Reading Research*, ed. R. Barr, M. L. Kamil, P. B. Mosenthal, and P. D. Pearson, 545–562. Mahwah, NJ: Lawrence Earlbaum Associates, Inc.

Pressley, M. 2002. Metacognition and self-regulated comprehension. In *What research has to say about reading instruction*. 3rd ed. Ed. A. E. Farstup, and S. J. Samuels, 291–309. Newark, DE: International Reading Association, Inc.

Pressley, M. 2002. Comprehension strategies instruction: A turn-of-the-century status report. In *Comprehension instruction: Research-based best practices,* ed. C. C. Block and M. Pressley, 11–27. New York: The Guilford Press.

Raphael, T. and K. Au. 2005. QAR: Enhancing comprehension and test taking across grades and content areas. *The Reading Teacher* 59(3): 206–221.

Readence, J. E., T. W. Bean, and R. S. Baldwin. 2000. *Content area literacy: An integrated approach.* Dubuque, IA: Kendall/Hunt Publishing Company.

Robb, L. 2003. *Teaching reading in social studies, mathematics and math.* New York: Scholastic.

Rupley, W. H., J. W. Logan, and W. D. Nichols. 1999. Vocabulary instruction in a balanced reading program. *The Reading Teacher* 52(4): 336–346.

Ryder, R. J. and M. F. Graves. 2003. *Reading and learning in content areas.* 3rd ed. New York: John Wiley & Sons, Inc.

Schwartz, R. M., and E. Raphael. 1985. Concept of definition: A key to improving students' vocabulary. *The Reading Teacher* 39(2): 198–205.

Smith, F. 2004. *Understanding reading: A psycholinguistic analysis of reading and learning to read.* Mahwah, NJ: Lawrence Erlbaum Associates.

Snowball, D. n.d. Comprehension for all. *Teaching PRE k–8: The Magazine for Professional Development.* http://www.teachingk-8.com/archives/articles/comprehension_for_all_by_diane_snowball.html.

Trabasso, T., and E. Bouchard. 2002. Teaching readers how to comprehend text strategically. In *Comprehension instruction: Research-based best practices*, ed. C. C. Block and M. Pressley, 176–200. New York: The Guilford Press.

Vacca, R. T., and J. L Vacca. 2005. *Content area reading: Literacy and learning across the curriculum.* 8th ed. Boston: Pearson Education, Inc.

West, C. K., J. A. Farmer, and P. M. Wolff. 1991. *Instructional design: Implications from cognitive mathematics.* Upper Saddle River, NJ: Prentice Hall.

Wood, K. D. 2002. Differentiating reading and writing lessons to promote content learning. In *Improving comprehension instruction: Rethinking research, theory, and classroom practice*, ed. C. C. Block, L. B. Gambrell, and M. Pressley, 155–180. Hoboken, NJ: John Wiley & Sons, Inc.

# References for Further Reading

Afflerbach, P. 2002. Teaching reading self-assessment strategies. In *Comprehension instruction: Research-based best practices*, ed. C. C. Block and M. Pressley, 96–111. New York: The Guilford Press.

Alexander, P. A., and T. L. Jetton. 2000. Learning from text: A multidimensional approach. In vol. 3 of *Handbook of Reading Research*, ed. R. Barr, M. L. Kamil, P. B. Mosenthal, and P. D. Pearson, 285–310. Mahwah, NJ: Lawrence Earlbaum Associates, Inc.

Bean, T. 2000. Reading in the content areas: Social constructivist dimensions. In vol. 3 of *Handbook of Reading Research*, ed. R. Barr, M. L. Kamil, P. B. Mosenthal, and P. D. Pearson, 629–644. Mahwah, NJ: Lawrence Earlbaum Associates, Inc.

Clark, S. K., C. Dugan, T. Moreine, J. O. Prior, J. Ray, M. Rosenburg, and A. Tischitta. 2004. *Successful Strategies for Reading in the Content Areas: Secondary*. Huntington Beach, CA: Shell Educational Publishing.

Duffy, G. 2002. The case for direct explanation of strategies. In *Comprehension instruction: Research-based best practices*, ed. C. C. Block and M. Pressley, 28–41. New York: The Guilford Press.

Guthrie, J. T. and A. Wigfield. 2000. Engagement and motivation in reading. In vol. 3 of *Handbook of Reading Research*, ed. R. Barr, M. L. Kamil, P. B. Mosenthal, and P. D. Pearson, 403–422. Mahwah, NJ: Lawrence Earlbaum Associates, Inc.

Ivey, G. 2002. Building comprehension when they're still learning to read the words. In *Comprehension instruction: Research-based best practices*, ed. C. C. Block and M. Pressley, 234–246. New York: The Guilford Press.

Keene, E. O. and S. Zimmermann. 1997. *Mosaic of Thought: Teaching Comprehension in a Reader's Workshop*. Portsmouth, NH: Heinemann.

Morrow, L. M. 2003. Motivating lifelong voluntary reading. In *Handbook of research on teaching the english language arts*, ed. J. Flood, D. Lapp, J. R. Squires, and J. M. Jensen, 857–867. Mahwah, NJ: Lawrence Erlbaum Associates, Publishers.

Ong, F, ed. 2000. *Strategic teaching and learning: Standards-based instruction to promote content literacy in grades four through twelve*. Sacramento, CA: California Department of Education.

Pardo, L. S. 2004. What every teacher needs to know about comprehension. *The Reading Teacher* 58(3): 272–280.

Parker, C. E. 2006. *30 Graphic Organizers for Reading Grades 3–5*. Huntington Beach, CA: Shell Educational Publishing.

Parker, C. E. and J. Dustman. 2005. *30 Graphic Organizers for Reading Grades K-3*. Huntington Beach, CA: Shell Educational Publishing.

Sinatra, G. M., K. J. Brown, and R. E. Reynolds. 2002. Implications of cognitive resource allocation for comprehension strategies instruction. In *Comprehension instruction: Research-based best practices*, ed. C. C. Block and M. Pressley, 62–76. New York: The Guilford Press.

Smolkin, L. B. and C. A. Donovan. 2002. 'Oh Excellent, Excellent Question!': Developmental Differences and Comprehension Acquisition. In *Comprehension instruction: Research-based best practices*, ed. C. C. Block and M. Pressley, 140–157. New York: The Guilford Press.

Tracey, D. H. and L. M. Morrow. 2002. Preparing young learners for successful reading comprehension. In *Comprehension instruction: Research-based best practices*, ed. C. C. Block and M. Pressley, 219–233. New York: The Guilford Press.

Vacca, R. T. 2002. Making a difference in adolescents' school lives: Visible and invisible aspects of content area reading. In *What research has to say about reading instruction*. 3rd ed. Ed. A. E. Farstup and S. J. Samuels, 184–204. Newark, DE: International Reading Association, Inc.

Wade, S. E. and E. Moje. 2000. The role of text in classroom learning. In vol. 3 of *Handbook of Reading Research*, ed. R. Barr, M. L. Kamil, P. B. Mosenthal, and P. D. Pearson, 609–628. Mahwah, NJ: Lawrence Earlbaum Associates, Inc.

Yopp, R. H. and H. K. Yopp. 2000. Sharing informational text with young children. *The Reading Teacher* 53:410–423. Newark, DE: International Reading Association.